Hannah Wood
of Blue Hill, Maine

Hannah Wood

Hannah Wood of Blue Hill, Maine

Reminiscences of an 1850 Childhood

Esther E. Wood

Genealogy House
Amherst, Massachusetts

Hannah Wood of Blue Hill, Maine
Reminiscences of an 1850 Childhood
by Esther E. Wood

Originally published 1982 as
Hannah: Reminiscences of an 1850 Childhood
by Esther E. Wood

Cover image: Library of Congress, Geography and Map Division

Genealogy House edition first published 2014

ISBN: 978-1-887043-11-3

Genealogy House
a division of
White River Press
PO Box 3561
Amherst, MA 01004
www.genealogyhouse.net

Dedication

These stories were written specially for
Hannah's Grandchildren
Elinor, Austin, Conrad, Edna and Barbara

Contents

Foreword xi
Hannah's Family xiii
Neighborhood Map xiv

   1. The Family 1
   2. The Neighbors 16
   3. A Winter at Friend's Corner 25
   4. Father and Mother Ashore 42
   5. Journeys With the Captain 57
   6. Building the *Meridian* 66
   7. Flavilla 81
   8. Gran'sir's Boys 92
   9. At Home and Away 108
 10. The Music Master 116
 11. The Stover Sisters 126

Afterword 133
Acknowledgements 135
About the Author 137

Foreword

A decade ago Samuel Taylor of East Blue Hill suggested that I write about my Aunt Hannah's mid-nineteenth century childhood. Some of her stories were unrecorded; some were written in old diaries and letters. I am grateful to Mr. Taylor for his suggestion.

In preparation for writing about the mid-nineteenth century I read letters and journals written in that period. I read fiction of the 1840's and the 1850's. I read numerous biographies of New Englanders who were children in the mid-century. Writing about my aunt's childhood has been for me an adventure in social history.

I have exercised a writer's prerogative. I have omitted some stories because they did not fit into the chapter outlines. I have changed names; I have altered details. I have twice changed the order of events and twice shifted the locale of a happening. I chose to close the book with the date 1855. Sarah Miller was one of Aunt Hannah's dearest friends. I regret that I did not have the knowledge or the skill to tell the story of the Hannah-Sarah friendship.

I had intended that Hannah would be the heroine of my book. In rereading the chapters, I have discovered that Flavilla is often the heroine.

My great-grandparents and my grandparents died before I was born. But because Aunt Hannah and Uncle Arthur and Father talked so often about them, I feel that I knew them. As my aunt, uncle and father loved and admired them, so I love and admire them. Writing about them has been a labor of love.

Hannah's Family (to 1846)

1. Patience Tibbetts b. 1800 (d. 1828) 2. Louisa Billings b. 1802

M.

John S. Friend b. 1800

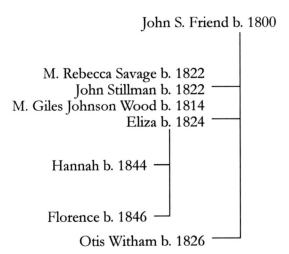

M. Rebecca Savage b. 1822
John Stillman b. 1822
M. Giles Johnson Wood b. 1814
Eliza b. 1824

Hannah b. 1844

Florence b. 1846
Otis Witham b. 1826

Blue Hill	to	McHeards

1 Peters' Place	A Peters' Mill
2 Stone House	B Doorstone Quarry
3 Isaac Saunders' House	C Grindle Quarry
4 Darling House	C1 Grindle Wharf
5 Zenas Closson's House	D Schoolhouse
6 Grindle House	E Spring
6A Grindle Barn	F Porgy Point
7 Friend House	G Joel Long Jr's Shipyard
7A Friend Barn	H Joel Long Jr's Sawmill
8 Robert Means' House	& Gristmill
(Elisha Day Place)	
	I McHeard's Schoolhouse
9 Hyer House	
10 Joel Long Sr.	
11 Joel Long Jr.	

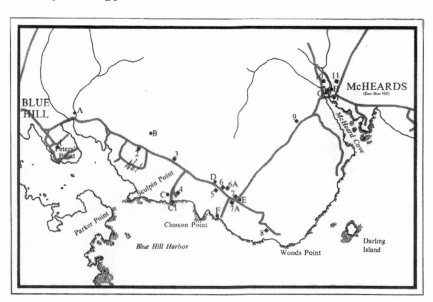

The Family

Grandfather John Friend was a young man when he came to the neighborhood that now bears his name. He bought the saltwater farm from the Widow Kimball. He brought his bride to the farm with him and settled down to a life of fishing and farming.

When I was a child I often said to Grandfather, "Tell me about your coming to the Corner." He always began his story the same way: "When I came here in 1821, there were no roads, only paths. One to the west went to the village; the one to the east went to McHeard's. When I went to either place, I rowed instead of walking. By boat the trip to the village was only about a mile. If I went round by way of the path, I had to walk two miles. I always like to go to town by boat, passing by the sharp points of land that jut out into the Bay, going through the Narrows to the inner Bay where the village with the mountain behind it is straight ahead. When I was young, nearly everyone went to the village by boat. I expect that is why the town center is called Head-of-the-Bay. Folks called the smaller village to the east McHeard's. McHeard was the first man to live on the stream there. One winter he broke his leg and was found frozen to death in his cabin."

"I always liked the trip back from the village. As I rowed home I could see the Falls, the Neck, and Harriman Point to my left with Long Island ahead. On clear days Mount Desert showed high and blue to the east of Long Island. After I had tied up my boat and climbed the steep pitch to the house, I turned to look back on the bay. It told me pretty well what the weather was going to be for the next few days. If I could see a sea glint, I knew that I would 'catch a wet skin'; if the sea was gray and choppy, I could count on a storm; if there was mist in the east, there would be fog on the morrow."

Grandfather told me that when he came to the Corner in 1821 there were only two dwelling houses between his house and the Head-of-the-Bay. The small farmhouse of Jonathan Darling was nearest. It was about a mile away, right near the shore. Mr. Darling's father had been one of the early settlers and built the first house on the east side of the Bay, below the Narrows. The second house was John Peters's. He had got ahead in the world by being miller, surveyor, and ship builder. On a point off the beaten path he had built a two-story brick house.

To the east of Grandfather's was the Elisha Day place. It was all woods from there to McHeard's Stream, where Joel Long, Sr. had put up a house that was part wood and part brick. Mr. Long made the bricks from clay on his own property. It is likely that he also made the bricks for the Peters' house.

The Kimball house that Grandfather had bought was a Cape Cod house with a large center chimney. It had five rooms below and two chambers above. Attached was a shed that was divided into a cheese room and a wood room. Upstairs was an unfinished chamber where pedlars were allowed to sleep and where Grandmother dried herbs. The downstairs bedroom belonged to Mrs. Kimball. Grandfather had agreed that she could live there and have the use of the kitchen. He promised to give her eggs, meat, milk, and vegetables.

Grandfather always liked to tell the story of how he came to meet Grandmother. I'd like to tell it to you. He was born in Sedgwick and was the second in a family of eleven children. His grandfather was Benjamin Friend, a first settler of the town. Benjamin's River is named for him.

One winter Grandfather went to Walker's Pond in Brooksville to frost-fish. When he got there he found three sisters skating on the ice. They were the oldest children of Captain John Tibbetts who lived near the Pond. When Grandfather saw the red cheeks and blue eyes of the second daughter and heard her gay laugh, he forgot all about fishing. He skated. After that he came to Brooksville often to see Patience Tibbetts.

The winter of their courtship was a sad one. In March the oldest sister, Eliza, and a neighbor were drowned when they started to cross the Pond on the ice. In the spring it was hard for Great-grandfather and Great-grandmother Tibbetts to let Patience marry and leave home. To make things easier for them a neighbor, Louisa Billings, came to live with them and help with the younger children.

Captain Tibbetts and his schooner brought Grandfather and his bride to the Kimball house. They sailed along Eggemoggin Reach and then into Western Blue Hill Bay. Patience brought her own flax wheel and spinning wheel and the quilts and rugs that she had made. Her mother had given her chairs and a tip-table. The Captain had donated a barrel of flour, a cask of salted mackerel, a jug of molasses, and a bag of coffee beans. Grandfather had some possessions; a scythe, a shovel, a spade, an axe, and an adze. His father had given him a cow, a bull, and several sheep. The animals were poor sailors and protested their voyage with bleats and baas.

The first summer, Patience was homesick. She missed seeing Cape Rosier, gathering water lilies on the pond, and being with her young brothers and sisters. Grandpa pointed out the view of Mount Desert and the blueness of the bay. He talked to her about clearing land for fields and pastures, building a new barn, and buying cattle to stock the farm. He promised that a road would soon be built between McHeard's and the village and that folks would move into the neighborhood. "At night you will be able to see lights," he said.

Grandfather recalled that his bride and the Widow Kimball became good friends. Very soon the Widow was eating all her meals with the family and had taken over the household knitting and mending. She liked to have a cup of tea in the mid-afternoon. After dinner she brewed a pot. When she went to her own room for an afternoon of sewing and resting, she took the pot with her, wrapped it in an old shawl, and put it under the bedclothes to keep the tea hot as long as possible. The household had two teapots; the bride's new one and the old under-the-quilts pot that belonged to Mrs. Kimball.

The Widow Kimball loved children. She only had five of her own, and she was always saying to Grandmother, "Have just as many babies as you can and have them as fast as you can." She was pleased when children were born the second and third years of the Friends' marriage. She carried for John Stillman, Eliza and Otis while their mother washed and cooked and cleaned.

After her children were born, Grandma Patience was no longer homesick. Her older sister and Louisa Billings came to make long visits; her mother spent one winter with her; Grandfather's younger sisters, Abigail and Hannah, came to stay one summer. The following year the Friend sisters married Joel Long, Jr., and his brother Charles and came to live at McHeard's.

She was pleased, too, when Grandfather built his barn, using beams, boards, shingles, and clapboards made from timber cut on his woodlot. He was an exact man. He laid out the barn and had each corner square with a point of the compass. About fifteen years later, when the road was built straight between the house and the barn, the barn set catercornered to the road. Folks used to laugh and call it "Friend's crooked barn." Grandfather was quick to defend his building: "A barn whose northern corner points straight to the North Star is not crooked." I've played and worked hours in Grandfather's barn, and it never seemed out of kilter to me.

Grandmother had another child in 1828. Both she and the new baby died. The next year was sad and difficult for Grandfather. He was lost without his young wife. The Widow Kimball died at about the same time. His sister Eunice came to keep house for him. She did not like housework and was unhappy there. The summer was very dry; rust and frost hit his crops; lightning injured an ox. His little boys were quarrelsome and his little girl, frail and complaining.

Grandfather was lonely. He often took the children to Brooksville to see their Tibbetts grandparents. It was not long before he began to take notice of Louisa Billings. He admired her capable ways and her good judgment. The following year he married her. He always said, "Good times walked through the door when I brought Louisa home with me."

Otis was seven years old when his stepmother became one of the family. I have often heard him tell of her coming: "The first thing she did after she took off her hat and coat was to give Eliza and me a stick of candy and to make John a sugar treat. Then she said, 'Wait 'til

I get my apron on, I'm going to get you a supper that will make your mouths water."

Uncle Otis told me that his stepmother asked the boys to call her Louisa, and they did. She often said to them, "I want you to always remember that Patience was your mother." Daily she spoke to them of Patience. She praised their mother's beauty, told them stories of her gaiety, and recalled the details of a childhood that the two of them had shared.

Grandma Louisa gave the house a great cleaning. She painted Mrs. Kimball's old room and made it into a bedroom for herself and Grandfather. In it she placed a high bed and a heavy bureau that had belonged to her grandmother. In the corner cupboard she arranged her gold-banded dishes. She added a sofa and rugs and chairs to the scanty Friend furnishings. But she was not too busy with the house to help with the farm. She took over the milking of the cows; she weeded the garden; she raked the hay; she helped pile the wood in the shed.

Whether at work in the house or on the farm, Grandpa's new wife liked to have her stepchildren near her. John and Otis became less quarrelsome; Eliza grew well and happy. Grandma was delighted that John Stillman and Eliza looked like their mother, and she used to say of her second stepson, "Otis may look like the Friends but he is Patience's son. He has her good humor and gaiety."

When the town set up a school district in the neighborhood, Grandmother offered to have school held in her front room and suggested that she board the master. The teacher that Mother and my uncles remembered best was Alan Wood. He had a cork leg, and the boys loved to stick pins in it. One day a careless boy rammed a pin into the wrong leg and got a good strapping. The leather strap was then a part of a teacher's equipment—as important as the slates and the books. Mr. Wood liked to tell his pupils the details of how Dr. Tenney removed his infected leg. Alan was stretched out on the kitchen table, drugged with whiskey, and held down by his father and uncle while the doctor sawed away. His father wrapped the cut off leg in a sheet and buried it at the foot of the Tolman Sweet apple tree. The schoolmaster always ended his story with the remark, "And you can see the tree today. It's the first apple tree on the left as you go up the lane to father's house."

My Uncle Otis liked to repeat to me the story of the master's leg and he gave the yarn an addition of his own: "I expect, Hannah, that if we were to go to the Wood lane today we'd see the imprint of that leg on the trunk of the tree." Whenever he and I went to the Head-of-the-Bay, I suggested that we visit the old apple tree, but he would put me off: "No time today but next time we'll go and see the imprint."

When the Friend children were older, they went to school at McHeard's as there was no winter term at Friend's Corner. Later, all three went to the Academy at the village. It was there that Eliza, my mother, met Giles Wood. He was a village boy who went as cook on local schooners. During the winter he took time off to go to the Academy, where he studied geometry, surveying, and navigation. But I don't believe he ever studied spelling. My, he was a poor speller.

Mother never talked about Father's courting of her, but Father did. How often have I heard him say, "Eliza Wood was the prettiest girl in school. She could have had the pick of the village boys—a Holt or a Darling or a Peters. But she took me, only a ship's cook." They were married in 1842 when Mother was eighteen and Father was twenty-eight. By that time he had worked his way up to first mate of a schooner. In a few years he became the captain. In sailor's lingo, working up from cook to captain is called "coming in through the hawse hole." Because Father was away at sea most of the time, Mother lived with Grandfather and Grandmother. I was born in November of 1844 and named for Father's sister. Florence was born in 1846.

Father never talked much about his childhood but there was one story he told over and over. One cold winter afternoon he had been sent to the grocery story to buy a gallon of molasses and a gallon of rum. On the walk home, his hands became cold. To dull the ache he kept changing the jugs from one hand to the other. In one of the transfers he dropped the rum jug on the frozen ground. It broke, and the rum poured down a rut into the ditch. Although he was twelve years old, he cried. He knew what would happen to him when he got home—and it did.

I never saw my Wood grandparents. They died before I was born. Father had his own sister, Hannah, two half-sisters, Sally and Roxanna, and two half-brothers, Nahum and Isaiah, who went to California at the time of the Gold Rush. Sometime I'll tell you about them.

Most of my recollections of the first six years of my life are about my little sister, Florence, who had long yellow curls. I remember that we used to wade in the meadow brook. It was there that she caught her death of cold. After she died, Grandfather and Grandmother prepared her body for burial and "laid her out" on their high bed. Father took me in his arms and carried me in to look at her. I still recall her waxen hands and long hair. Because Grandmother and Mother cried, I cried. But I really did not understand that we would never again wade in the brook.

After Florence died, my father thought that it would be a good idea for my mother to go to sea with him. He hoped that a voyage would help her get over her little girl's death. I have been told that Mother and Grandmother thought I should go too, but Father had said, "No. A schooner is too confining for a young child. If you ever go again, Eliza, perhaps then Hannah may come along."

Mother discovered that she loved going to sea. She was a better sailor than her husband. She was never seasick; he was always sick the first two or three days out. The long hours aboard ship gave her plenty of time for reading and writing. In every new port she got out her sketch book and made a picture of the harbor. She loved the excitement of seeing new places and meeting new people. So, instead of her trip of 1850 being her only voyage, it was the first of many. For a decade she went with Father on every trip, whether the schooner was bound for Portland or Port-au-Prince.

Before every trip my mother always urged me to go with them and Grandmother sided in with her. Par Giles was willing for me to go along. Grandfather never said anything, but just before sailing time he would start a project in his workshop. When I was very small, he started a doll's cradle or a cart or a set of doll's furniture; when I was older, he would begin working on a lapdesk or shoes or a stool. One year he put up two swings in the barn. When I asked him about them, he said, "I plan to ask Flavilla Billings over for a few months. If you decide to stay at home, we shall need two swings."

On the day before the schooner sailed Par Giles would ask me, "What do you say, Hannah? Are you coming with us?" My reply was always the same: "Not this time, I'm going to stay with Grandpa and Grandma. They need me."

The folks took my refusal with smiles. Grandmother always looked sharply at her husband. Once I heard her say to him after Mother and Father had left the room, "John Friend, I hope that you never stoop to bribery."

I often think of Grandfather and Grandmother. I like to recall them as they looked in my childhood. Both had been born in 1800. Both were rugged and well in the 1850s.

Grandfather had become bald but his face had few wrinkles. He had sharp features and very blue eyes. He was not a tall man. He moved slowly—I don't remember that he ever ran or hurried. Grandfather had a speech mannerism. He spoke softly and very, very slowly. When he was asked a question, he was so slow to answer that usually the speaker repeated his query. Grandmother was annoyed by his slowness and she often prodded him, "Speak up, John, do or we shall think that you have lost either your ears or your tongue."

Grandmother was as tall as Grandfather. She had a round, full face and mass of gray hair that she piled high on her head in a braided pug. In her girlhood she had had her ears pierced and she always wore gold earrings and gold beads. Her hands were always busy. Even when she sat down to rest, she mended or knitted. She spoke quickly and came to decisions quickly. Uncle Otis used to say, "Louisa can make up her mind and then have time to help Father make up his."

From the time I was six until I was twelve Uncle Otis lived with his parents, so of course I knew him very well. Smaller, darker, and less handsome than his brother John, he was the favorite son. Indeed, he was everyone's favorite, for he was good-natured and full of fun. He played the fiddle, the trumpet, and the drum. Where he was, there was laughter. He insisted on doing the hardest work on the farm. He also helped in the kitchen and learned to knit so that he could lighten Grandma's load of mitten-making.

Uncle Otis was always telling me nonsense that I believed. Once I asked him, "Why does Grandma have gray eyes when all the rest of us have blue ones?"

He replied, "Her eyes were once blue but they faded out because she had to keep such a sharp lookout on brother John, your mother, and me."

Another time I questioned him about my grandfather's slowness of speech. He gave an explanation that I believed for years: "When he was a small boy, Father was scared by twin hoot owls and he never got over it."

Uncle Otis liked to teach me tongue-twisters. I mastered all the P's in the Peter Piper story and all the B's in the saga of Betty Barter and the bitter butter. He once suggested that I repeat one of them to Elder Gilpatrick and challenge him to recite it. Soon thereafter, the Elder came to supper. He had hardly said the blessing before I "ribbled off" the lines, "Betty Barter bought a box of bitter butter. A box of bitter butter Betty Barter bought. Betty put the bitter butter in the batter and the bitter butter made the batter bitter." Then I declared, "I'll bet you can't say that, Elder."

He couldn't, but he turned the tables on me and said, "I'll bet, Hannah, that you cannot repeat the names of the books of the Old Testament."

I couldn't, but Grandma had me memorize them before the Elder came again to supper.

Uncle Otis was twice married in the 1840s and for a time lived away from the Corner. His wives were never mentioned in the family nor were his six years of absence referred to. Grandfather and Grandmother called him "our unmarried son." Grandfather deferred to his judgment in the planning of the farm work. Now and then Uncle went to Brooksville to visit his Tibbetts aunts and uncles. Then his stepmother said, "The sun never shines as bright when Otis is away."

Now I'll tell you about my mother. I have heard Grandmother often say, "Eliza looks like her brother John Stillman but she acts like her brother Otis." Mother wore her yellow hair in curls over her forehead and ears. She was sensitive about her large ears and took pains to cover them. Her eyes were very blue and her pink cheeks flushed easily. The surprise of finding a hen's nest in the orchard or the expectation of having company or the excitement of packing for a voyage all brought color to her face.

Mother had her own way of doing things. Her way was not the orderly, deliberate way of her father, or the efficient, well planned way of her stepmother. She did things "when the spirit moved." She left her bed unmade if she chose to go walking; she hid the mending in the closet if she wished to go berrying. When a new book or magazine or paper came into the house, she ignored her household chores. She preferred gardening, cutting clippings, and reading to sewing, sweeping, and cooking.

The flower beds at Grandfather's were hers, and when she was at home from sea she gave them enthusiastic care. When she gardened, mother pinned her skirts and petticoats to her knees. She shoveled and wheeled manure; she dug up and reset plants; she edged the borders with shells that she had brought from the south. When she finished, she took off her shoes and lay in the sun.

As I grew older I realized that my mother was different from the mothers of my best friends, Abbey Saunders and Sarah Miller. Their mothers did not run races with children or climb trees to look in birds' nests. They did not memorize pages and pages of poetry and sit up all night to finish reading a book. They did not get up at four o'clock to watch a June sunrise or go out for a walk in a thunderstorm.

I never knew my grandparents or my father to try to change Mother's ways. Once when I was older, I said to Father, "You should keep Mother from going to walk in a storm." He replied, "I couldn't. You should know by this time that she is a law unto herself."

My father was not a tall man but he appeared tall because he stood straight and carried his head very high. He had a wide forehead and large blue eyes. His blond hair and his under-chin beard were thick and well trimmed. He liked to dress up and delighted in his velvet cravats and flowered waistcoats. He was regretful that Mother did not care for finery. Par Giles was also an affectionate man. When I was a child he often said to me, "Hannah, I love you a lot. Kiss me quick!" He called my mother "darling" and referred to my grandmother as "dear Louisa." He used to say to his father-in-law, "Mr. Friend, I love you as though you were my father."

He spoke to every stranger whom he met, whether the man were pastor or pedlar. I never knew anyone who liked to shake hands as much as he did. When we went to church or to prayer meeting, he never left for home until he had spoken to every man, woman, and child there and shaken each by the hand. Uncle Otis used to laugh at Father's cordiality. "Giles," he said, "would have made a great politician." But Father's affection for people was real, and others seemed to sense that.

Father liked to talk in public. It gave him pleasure to testify at prayer meeting and to speechify at town meeting. He was proud to be a Baptist and a Whig. He had a beautiful tenor and could sing gospel hymns and sea chanteys with equal enjoyment.

He liked a hearty joke, especially one on himself. Father had what Uncle called "a belly laugh": when he laughed, we could hear him all over the house.

He was also a practical joker. Grandmother always wore an apron—calico in the morning, white lawn in the afternoon. When she was seated in a chair, Father liked to steal up behind her, untie the bow of the apron strings, and then tie the strings to the back of the chair so that when Grandmother stood, up came the chair with her. In the evenings he often made molasses candy—the pulled kind. After the long strips had hardened, he cut them into pieces, then summoned the cat and Painter, the dog, to the kitchen. On the roof of the mouth of each he pressed a piece of the sticky candy. The sweet lump remained there until it was lapped away. Cat and dog sat either side of the stove and lapped and lapped and lapped. Grandfather watched their annoyed expressions and their energetic tongue movements and he laughed and laughed and laughed.

Long after we had eaten the candy, (and the poor animals had disposed of their lumps), Father's mouth continued to twitch and his eyes to sparkle with fun. One evening I said to him, "Par Giles, why do you look so happy?" Before he could answer, Mother answered for him, "Your father not only looks happy, Hannah. He is happy. Remember that the Good Book says, 'A merry heart maketh a cheerful countenance.'"

John Stillman Friend, my older uncle, had left home before I was born, but he often came to visit. He was tall, blond, and very handsome. Grandfather and Grandma Louisa agreed that he looked like his mother,

Patience. He was proud appearing and always dignified. He had married Rebecca Savage and lived in a big house in Blue Hill village. Uncle John went as first mate on a Portsmouth, New Hampshire, ship that was in the China trade. When he came to visit at the Corner, he found it hard to talk to his folks, for he was not interested in farming and he did not like to talk about his voyages. His wife seldom came with him. I noticed that when she did come, Grandmother got out a linen cloth and set the table with the best dishes. Otis used to ask, "Why do you put on style, Louisa? The Savages are no better than the Friends."

Otis was the only one in the family who did not stand in awe of Rebecca. He liked to jolly her about not going to sea with her husband. Once at the supper table, he said to her, "What kind of a captain's wife will you be, Rebecca, if you don't go to sea? Better go while John is the first mate. It is time that you got used to the roll of a ship."

Uncle Otis's remark seemed to give courage to John Stillman, and for once he spoke up to his wife, "If you don't come with me this time, Rebecca, you may never have another chance."

Rebecca set her cup down so hard that she slopped the tea on the cloth. "Otis, I tire of your jokes," she said. Then she turned on her husband: "John Stillman, of course I'll have another chance. The new ship will make it to China and back, and nothing is going to happen to you. In a year and a half you'll be back pestering me about going to sea again. We'll see about it when the time comes. But I do say right now that a ship never brought good fortune to a Savage."

John Stillman was silent, but Uncle Otis remarked loudly and clearly, "May I remind you, Rebecca, that you are no longer a Savage. You are a Friend."

I noticed that after this exchange of words, only Uncle Otis and I enjoyed the supper. Nothing ever interfered with Uncle's appetite and I did not understand what the talk was all about.

During the first winter that Mother went to sea with Par Giles, my grandparents and I went to call on Aunt Rebecca. It was my grandmother's idea. "'It is only fitten and proper that we go to see John Stillman's wife," she said. "Don't count on me going," replied Uncle.

I could see that Grandfather did not really wish to go. For several weeks he made excuses: Brownie was overworked; the sledding was poor; he himself was all tuckered out. Finally Grandma took things into her hands. On Thursday she said, "John, I plan to go to see Rebecca this Saturday. If you can't arrange to take Hannah and me, I'll ask Mr. Grindle to take us."

Grandfather ruefully agreed to go. We took our baths a day early. On Friday evening a roaring fire was built in the kitchen stove, the wooden wash tub was set in front of the opened oven door, and the tub was filled with hot water from the stove tank. Grandfather and Uncle went into the front room while Grandmother bathed me and took her own bath. Clean clothing was laid out for the morning and we put on fresh woolen nighties. When my bath was over, I ran into the cold bedroom and jumped into my trundle bed, which was warmed by two soapstones, one for my feet and one for my back. I was asleep before Grandfather and Uncle had finished their baths.

The next morning, Grandmother did not do her usual Saturday baking in the brick oven. She was eager to have an early dinner and get our clothes changed for our trip to town. She took special pains with my hair and put my new red dress on me. She and Grandfather wore their Sunday clothes.

There was considerable discussion about a present for Aunt Rebecca. Uncle remarked, "No need to take a thing." Grandmother suggested giving her two coin spoons but Grandfather was firm: "That I will not allow. The spoons must be kept for Eliza and Hannah." They compromised on taking a ham and a container of maple syrup.

Brownie had been given a day of rest on Friday in preparation for his journey to the village. He seemed to enjoy pulling the sleigh over the snow-covered roads, but when he came to Tenney Hill where Aunt Rebecca lived, he slowed to a walk. Aunt occupied one side of a two-and-a-half-story house with a great central chimney. Her sister, who had married a Darling, lived in the other half. Brownie did not want to turn into the drive, just as though he sensed his owner's diffidence at making the call. Once in the driveway, he stepped quickly to the hitching post, where Grandfather fastened him and took care to unfasten the check rein and to cover him with a horse blanket and our warm lap robe. Just before we knocked at the door Grandpa said, "We can't stay long. I don't want Brownie to get chilly."

Aunt Rebecca opened the door. She was a tall woman with black hair and eyes. She invited us in, helped us off with our coats, and led us into her sitting room. The door to the parlor was shut, and I longed to see what was behind the closed door. Grandfather placed the gifts on the table and we sat down. Grandma and I sat on the horsehair sofa. It was so slippery that I kept sliding off and Grandma had to reseat me.

Finally Aunt Rebecca said, "Hannah, you may go to the whatnot and look at the shells but do not touch them."

I was glad to get down from the sofa and was pleased to look at the shell collection. There were brown shells, white shells, and pink shells. There was a mother-of-pearl shell. Some were large and some were very small. There was a small pink shell with a white interior. I longed to touch it and to hold it in my hand. I thought how wonderful it would be to own it and take it home and put it on the kitchen shelf. I was so taken up with the shell collection that I did not hear what my elders were talking about, though now and then I heard them refer to John Stillman and Salem and Canton.

After a little while Mrs. Darling came into the room. She was blonde and plump and smiling. She shook Grandfather's hand, kissed Grandmother's cheek, and put her arm over my shoulder. "I was looking for a little girl to eat some new cookies and to look at the black kittens in the kitty-basket," she said. I needed no urging to go to her kitchen with her. She pulled up a chair to the kitchen table for me, placed a kitten in my lap, and shared a plate of cookies with me. There were red geraniums in bloom on the windowsills. She talked about her plants and showed me the rug that she was making. The rug had a spotted dog pattern and she was hooking W E L C O M E below the figure of the dog. I talked about Brownie and the cows and the partridge in the russet tree. Finally I told her about the pink shell and how I would love to hold it in my hand. "You shall," she said, "Come back into Rebecca's sitting room. But you'll have to leave the kitten here. My sister won't have cats in her half of the house."

When we were back in the sitting room, she pulled a footstool in front of the whatnot and handed me the pink shell saying, "I want Hannah to hold the shell. She won't hurt it." For the duration of our stay I held the shell. I clutched it so hard that it became hot and sticky.

The longer I held it, the more I wanted it. I thought of how I would take it to bed with me and put it under my pillow if only it were mine.

When my grandparents got up to leave, Grandmother said, "Hannah, give the shell to your Aunt Rebecca." I wanted to say, "Do I have to?" But my aunt held out her hand for the shell. She took it, wiped it with her handkerchief, and replaced the shell on the whatnot. Mrs. Darling started to speak: "Rebecca, couldn't you —" but a glance from her sister silenced her.

We went into the hall, put on our coats, and left. I noticed how quickly Aunt Rebecca shut the door after us. So did Grandfather and Grandmother. Grandmother tried to excuse her daughter-in-law's haste; "She shut the door quickly so as to keep out the cold." We were at the sleigh before my grandfather got out his reply: "No, I think that she was in a hurry to get back in the sitting room and count the shells."

Grandfather was just turning Brownie from the driveway into the road when we heard someone calling to us. It was Mrs. Darling. She had thrown a red shawl over her head and was running toward us. She thrust into my hand a purple and brown shell saying, "Hannah, I want you to have this shell that your Uncle John Stillman gave me. I really do not like it. Purple is not my color." Without waiting for my thanks she ran back into the house. I put the shell inside my mitten and held it in the palm of my hand. All the way home I thought about my new possession and where I should keep it.

I noticed that my grandparents were unusually quiet. They hardly said a word. Finally as we turned Peters' Corner my grandfather spoke, speaking even more slowly and softly than was his want, "I guess my son chose the wrong sister." Grandmother's reply was neither soft nor slow: "John Friend, never let me hear you talk like that again!"

When we got home, Grandmother took Uncle Otis aside. I heard her say to him, "Please don't ask your father about our visit to Rebecca's. I noticed that she cooked "pudding" for Grandpa's supper and placed a pitcher of sweet cream beside his bowl. I thought that my grandfather looked sad, so I put my little purple shell right beside his teacup.

The Neighbors

By the time of my childhood a road had been built between the village and McHeard's. Grandpa used to say that the road was just as crooked as the path had been. Four new houses had been built in our neighborhood. Our nearest neighbor was Milford Grindle, who had bought the house of Anson Darling's widow. It was a large Cape Cod house with a beautiful fan doorway. It had been built just before I was born. Captain Darling, his son, and all hands aboard were lost when their ship went down in the Bay of Chaleur when returning from Spain with a load of salt for the fishing fleet.

Captain Darling and my father were like the other Blue Hill men of their generation. They had been brought up on saltwater farms. They knew how to plant and tend a garden, how to cut and make hay and how to butcher and "put down" meat. They could go into the woods, cut trees, and measure up cordwood. They took grain to the gristmill and timber to the sawmill. They knew how to stretch nets for catching porgies in midsummer, and how to cut holes in the ice for frost-fishing in deep winter. Often they knew about surveying and blacksmithing and building. When they went to sea they became "Sams-of-all-skills": they could cook lobscouse in the galley or reef a sail aloft or set the ship's course at the wheel.

Milford Grindle belonged to a later generation than did Anson Darling and Giles Wood. He had all the farm skills that they had but he never went to sea. Instead, he combined farming with quarrying. He "got out" paving for city streets, hired men to work in the quarry holes, and built a large barn to house the oxen that drew the loads of paving. He "threw up" a wharf of waste stone and from it he shipped paving to ports as far away as New Orleans. Milford Grindle was what

Grandfather called "a hustler." A small, nimble man with a very loud voice, he was always shouting at his horse or the cows or the oxen but he never raised his hand to strike them. When he shouted, we could hear him way over to our house.

I was eleven when Mr. Grindle and his wife Belinda had their first baby. I liked to go over and rock little Elva. At first I was frightened of Mr. Grindle, for all the people in my family were softspoken. But Mrs. Grindle put me at ease. "Don't mind my husband," she said, "he is all bluster and no bite."

Mr. Grindle did like his cup of strong, hot tea in summer or in winter. When he was driving his ox team home from the quarry, he would pause at the crest of the hill a quarter of a mile from his house and bellow, "Belinda, brew the tea!" After he had reached home and put the creatures in the barn, he would rush into the kitchen shouting, "Where's my tea? Where's my tea?" It was always in the teapot. Belinda poured her tea into a cup, but her husband drank his from the spout of the pot. This seemed to me a peculiar way to take tea, and I once said to Mrs. Grindle, "I don't think that Grandma Louisa would let Grandpa drink his tea that way." She replied, "Likely not, dear. My husband is so kind in ways that count that I overlook his little oddities."

Mr. Grindle kept an ugly horse, Old Gyp. The master and the horse understood each other perfectly. The master knew that a raised hoof did not mean a kick was coming, that bared teeth did not mean a bite was in prospect. The horse knew that shouts and threats were never followed by blows. When Gyp was not in use, he had the run of the farm, and he was the terror of tramps and foot pedlars who more than once had suffered from his blows and nips. The horse knew the neighbors and never touched us, but he would put back his ears and show the whites of his eyes as though to say, "I'm a one-man horse, Milford Grindle's horse."

Zenas Closson's house was down the hill from the Grindle place and on the opposite side of the road. It was built end to the street with a basement kitchen, like the houses that Mr. Closson had known when he had worked in Boston. He had not liked the city. Early in the 1840s he had brought his young family home to Blue Hill, bought land from his brother-in-law, Captain Darling, built a house, and started farming.

When I was very young, Grandmother and I went to call on the Clossons. I looked at Mr. Closson and was frightened. He was a tall, broadshouldered man with red hair and beard, and he reminded me of the picture of Jeremiah that was in my book of Bible stories. When he spoke to me, I was even more frightened and hid my face in Grandmother's lap. He had a hair lip and a cleft palate. His mustache covered the scar on his upper lip but there had been no operation to help his speech trouble.

Mr. Closson understood how I felt. He allowed Mrs. Closson and Grandmother to do the talking. After a little time, he got up and left the kitchen. When he came back, he brought me a cup that he had made of birch bark and filled with ripe, red strawberries. He handed the cup to me but did not speak. Grandmother prompted me: "Come, Hannah, thank Mr. Closson for the nice present." Before I could answer, the man said very softly to my grandmother, "Please ask Hannah to call me Uncle Zenas. I want all the young ones at the Corner to call me that."

Mr. Closson and Mr. Grindle were devoted friends though they were always formal when they spoke to each other. Mr. Closson had no oxen. When he needed a pair, he went to the Grindle barn, yoked up a pair, and drove them off to work. Often the owner of the oxen came from the quarry for an additional yoke. When he found the oxen gone, he stepped outside the barn and roared, "Mr. Closson, bring those critters back. I mean now." He shouted until he was breathless and then he went into the house to refresh himself with a few swigs from the teapot. Mr. Closson never chose to answer. He brought back the oxen when he had finished his work.

Our third neighbor lived nearly a mile to the west from Grandfather's. He was Isaac Saunders who had come from North Orland to work in the quarry. He had bought a small piece of land from Mr. Grindle and built a house and barn. His little girl Abbey was my age. When I was eight years old, Grandmother let me walk up to Saunders's to spend the afternoon. Sometimes we made mud pies at the brook; on hot afternoons we played with dolls in the shade of the lilacs.

One afternoon when I was coming home from Abbey's, I had an adventure and it was not a happy one. I had just passed the trail leading to the quarry and the wharf when I saw a large ram grazing by the roadside. The ram saw me. In a moment he was after me. I ran hard and climbed a high rock where I was out of reach of his sharp horns. He went back to feeding. After a little while I got off the rock with the hope that he had forgotten about me. He had not. Time and again, I tried to escape and he drove me back to the rock.

At first I did not mind my captivity. I looked around at the wild flowers and could see roses and primroses and butter-and-eggs. I counted the pines that I could see. (There were twelve.) High trees hid the bay but I could hear the gulls quarreling on the shore. Once, I saw a fish hawk fly over. A woodpecker beat a tattoo on a dead birch in back of me.

For awhile I entertained myself by repeating verses:

> How pleasant is Saturday night
> When I've tried all the week to be good,
> When I've spoken up for the right,
> And done all of the work that I could.

******

> It is not all in bringing up
> Let folks say what they will.
> Silver wash a pewter cup.
> It will be pewter still.

> It is not all in bringing up
> Let folks say what they will.
> Neglect may dim a silver cup,
> It will be silver still.

Then I started to wonder who would come to rescue me from the ram. I knew that it would not be Grandfather and Grandmother, for they had gone to Long's gristmill. I knew that it would not be Uncle Otis, for he was in the back field hoeing potatoes. I hoped that a traveler from the village would come along, but as the shadows started to lengthen and no one came, I despaired and started to bawl. I cried so hard that I annoyed the ram and he kept raising his head to look at me.

The sun had almost set when at last I heard a voice. I looked up the stretch of road but no one was in sight. The voice grew louder, and I soon recognized it. It was Mr. Grindle's. I decided that he must be returning from work and was talking to his oxen. In a moment I knew differently. I could make out the words "Mr. Closson." I saw the big red oxen turn from the quarry trail on to the road. On their left walked their owner with a goad in his hand. He was talking loudly and continually. On their right walked Mr. Closson with bent head. He was listening and nodding.

At a glance the two neighbors took in my predicament. Mr. Closson ran to the rock and lifted me down. With a roar Mr. Grindle attacked the ram and chased him down the road. He drove the ram out of sight and then ran back to us shouting and talking all the way. "Poor Hannah!" he said, "You must ride in the cart or else let Uncle Zenas carry you home."

By that time I had wiped my eyes and recovered my dignity. "No, thank you," I said, "I would like to walk beside you and carry the goad stick."

At the top of the next hill, Mr. Grindle shouted "Whoah" to the oxen. They halted. He cupped his mouth with his hands and shouted, "Belinda, get out the milk and the cookies!"

The ram gave me a great scare but it all had a happy ending. My grandfather drove to his brother Robert's in Sedgwick and brought home a dog to protect me—a great black fellow that for the next eight years was my constant companion. Uncle Robert had named him Painter. The dogs in my reading books were called Rover or Fido. It took a little time for me to get used to my protector's name.

The fourth house in the neighborhood was the Means place. It was "under the hill," about a quarter of a mile from Grandfather's. It was right near the shore and had been built on the foundation of the Elisha Day dwelling. Captain Means and Par Giles were great friends. As young men they had sailed on the same schooner, Mr. Means as mate and my father as cook. They liked to joke with each other. Captain Means used to say to Father, "I don't know how good a captain you are, Giles, but I do know that when it comes to making plum duff and slumgullion you are A-Number-One."

Now, further east, very near the McHeard's settlement, on a hilltop that overlooked the harbor was the house of Mrs. Hyer. In my childhood she was a real old lady, or so she seemed to me. She was there before Grandfather Friend came to Blue Hill and it was the Widow Kimball that told Grandfather about her.

At the time of the War of 1812, she had walked into town with a baby strapped to her back. A Frenchwoman who spoke only broken English, she carried a small valise of clothing and called herself Mrs. Hyer. She had enough money to buy a plot of land, to have a house built, and to get food for herself and the child. Mrs. Hyer was dark; the baby was blond. She never told anyone about herself and the child. People guessed that the baby was not hers, that someone for some reason or other had paid her to take the child. It was thought that she came from Quebec Province. She did not give the child her name; she called him John Miller. He grew up and became a prosperous captain, and he took good care of his foster mother.

It was rumored that Mrs. Hyer had a way of earning a little money on her own. In the 1850s Maine adopted the "Maine Law" providing for state prohibition of alcohol. We were supposed to go dry but we didn't. Liquor was smuggled in from Canada and New Hampshire. In most every town there were a few people who were said to sell drink on the sly. People believed that Mrs. Hyer had illegal brew stored in her shed and that she sold it after dark to those who came with cash to pay for it.

I was eleven years old before I was allowed to walk to McHeard's alone and then only if Painter went with me. When I was younger, Grandmother and I used to walk down to call on Aunt Abigail. On the walk home I always liked to call on Mrs. Hyer. I never could understand why Grandmother was not eager to call. Usually, I had my way and we went into Mrs. Hyer's. She made delicious cup custards. In summer the four custards in cracked cups would be set to cool on a window sill. In winter they would be lined up on the shelf behind the kitchen stove. Mrs. Hyer always gave me a custard; once she gave me four. She had evidently been drinking something that made her confused. She gave me a cup of custard and a spoon. At once, I scraped off the crisp brown top and ate it. Suddenly Mrs. Hyer looked at my cup and exclaimed, "The poor little girl—I gave her a custard that was not well browned. Give that one to me. Here is another." After I had spooned off the topping of the second, she made the same commiserating remark and handed me custard number three. Grandmother was too polite to say anything, and to her consternation I ate the tops off of all four custards before we left for home.

When I was seven years old, I went to the district school in the Friend's Corner neighborhood. The small schoolhouse had been built opposite the Closson house. It had an iron stove in the middle of the room with a long stovepipe connecting it to the end chimney. On cold days the hot pipe helped to heat the room. Against three sides of the room were backless benches with narrow desks in front of them. The desks and the benches for the younger children were nearer the stove. There were windows on two walls only, the western and the southern.

Two little privies stood in back of the schoolhouse but on occasion the boys relieved themselves through the knotholes in the back wall. At recess time we liked to cross the road and use the Closson outhouse, for it was an elegant one with five holes graded for size and height. It was cleaned out every week and often scrubbed. At one end were hung several dozen dried fish. We liked to rip off pieces of the flesh, slip them into our pockets, and use them for an in-school tidbit.

Uncle Zenas did not object when we used his privy or sampled his dry fish. He expected us to fill the school pail at his well and to pick apples in his orchard. But he did look unhappy when we invaded his turnip patch to play "scalp the Indians." We imagined that the turnip tops resembled the top-knots of Indians and we scalped a good many of his turnips. He said nothing, though. Uncle Zenas was one to live at peace with all men—especially with children.

There was no blackboard in the schoolroom. Each scholar brought his own slate and books. I had the same readers that my uncles and my mother had used, but Father bought me a new history and geography. Grandmother covered them with brown cambric to save them from wear.

I knew the alphabet and could read a few words before I went to school. Abbey Saunders and I were seatmates and neither of us had trouble learning. I remember that Harrison Whitney did have trouble.

Perhaps he was not really interested in his lessons, and he was also full of mischief. I remember that one day the master picked him right off the floor and hung him from a wire hook on the stovepipe. Down came the boy and the pipe in a shower of ashes. School was dismissed for the rest of the day while the teacher cleaned up the room. One recess time Harrison teased me; quick as a wink, I seized the broom and hit him on the head with the handle. I really stunned him and he sat down on the door rock. That taught me a lesson about controlling my temper.

Our teachers were always masters, usually men who walked from the village in the morning and then home at the close of the school day. One time, Grandmother boarded a master for a spell, just as she had when her step-children were going to school. He said that it was the best boarding place he ever had because she served pie every day.

Heard Lord was the master whom I liked best. I made the most progress with him. He let Painter come into the schoolroom with me and you may be sure that Harrison Whitney did not then dare to pinch me or pull my hair. Mr. Lord always brought his harmonica with him, and when he saw that the children were getting tired, he said, "Now put away your books and we'll have a tune or two." He played while we sang the few songs that we knew. I was not much at singing, but Abbey had a beautiful treble voice. Sometimes the master and Joel Closson sang duets. "O SUSANNAH" was our favorite.

On pleasant days I walked home for the noon meal. On cold or stormy days Grandma wrapped a few biscuits and some cookies in a towel and I took my dinner to school. I liked that because I could eat with Abbey, who always brought her dinner to school. So did the Whitney children who lived nearly a mile from the schoolhouse. Their father quarried stone from the Doorstone Quarry.

There were never more than fifteen children in the school when I went there. The schoolroom would not have held many more, anyway. The girls and the boys did not play together at recess and noontime. While the boys quarreled, wrestled, and threw rocks at birds the girls "kept house" on the flat rock back of the schoolhouse or played games in the Closson yard. We had fun with puss-in-the-corner and drop-the-handkerchief. But we had problems when we played the latter because the boys were sure to steal the handkerchief. Some of the children remained after school to play, but I never did. I was eager to get back to the farm to see my grandfather and grandmother.

A Winter at Friend's Corner

The first winter that Mother went to sea with Par Giles I slept in my grandparents' bedroom. Grandfather got down the Widow Kimball's trundle bed from the shed chamber. Grandmother found two feather beds for it; I slept on one and under the other. In the daytime my trundle was pushed under the big bed. At bedtime it was pulled out beside my grandparents' bed so that during the night Grandma could reach down to feel if I were covered.

We got up early in the morning, long before it was light. Uncle Otis always built the kitchen fire and laid kindling and logs in the front room fireplace for later. We dressed in the kitchen—first Uncle, Grandfather and Grandmother next, and then I. Dressing meant putting on heavy caps, coats and mittens because we did the barn chores before we ate our breakfast. Uncle lighted two lanterns, one for himself and his father, the other for Grandmother and me.

The men went to the barn first. Before Grandmother and I went out she turned down the wick of the lamp and put a stick of wood on the fire. By the time we reached the barn, Grandfather and Uncle had cleaned out behind the cows and thrown the manure out the tie-up window. They had pitched down the hay for the oxen, for Brownie, the horse, and for the cows, Daisy and Buttercup. The Friend cows always had floral names. Later, Daisy and Buttercup were joined by Primrose and Clover.

It was Grandma's chore to milk the cows. She always said, "A cow lets down her milk better for a woman." Before she started to milk she hung the lantern on a wall nail so that its light fell on the cow's udder. She took a cloth from the pocket of her apron and carefully wiped the bag and the teats of the cow. Then she seated herself on the milking stool and with the pail steadied by her knees, began to milk. I sat near her and watched. With a teat in each hand, she squeezed and pulled, relaxed her grasp, then again squeezed and pulled. First she milked the teats nearest to her. When all four had been milked, she "stripped the cow" by giving each teat pressure and a quick pull that brought a final stream of milk into the pail.

I liked to listen to the sound of the milk when it struck the bottom of the empty pail. I liked to see the tiny splashes that the milk made in the full pail. I was not the only one who watched Grandma milk; the barn cats were watching, too. When the cows had been milked, Grandmother poured warm milk into two bowls that stood beside the grain bins. The cats were ready. They pushed their noses so deep into the bowls that their whiskers were bedaubed with foam.

Uncle carried the full pails back to the kitchen. Grandmother and I trudged after him. He put the pails in the buttery while Grandmother took off her own and my wraps and hurried to start breakfast. The oven was hot: into it she pushed the left-over supper biscuits. The coffee beans had been ground the night before. She measured four tablespoons of the coffee into the tin pot, filled it with cold water, and placed it on the stove to boil. She got out her iron spider, removed the stove lid, and placed the spider over the hot flames. We always had something fried for breakfast—eggs or bacon or sausage or pork steak. My part in getting breakfast was to bring the doughnuts from the cellarway. Grandma always gave me the same caution, "Hannah, take care not to fall down the stairs."

Grandma served pie for breakfast whenever the men were working all day in the woods. When she took out the hot biscuits, she shoved a pie into the oven, either mince or apple. Her comment was always the same, "Pie in the winter should be hot, red hot." If Uncle heard her, he was sure to say, "Pie in the winter should have cheese with it. Don't you remember, Hannah, the lines, 'Apple pie without the cheese is like the kiss without the squeeze?'"

Before Grandfather and Uncle went to work they had to water the stock. If it were not too cold, I went to the barn with them after Grandma had bundled me up in my outside things. If it were very cold, Uncle touched off the fire in the fireplace and I stood beside a front window and watched. Grandmother insisted that even there I must wear my coat and cap. She scraped a peek-hole through the frost on the pane and gave the order, "Hannah, keep your hands off the cold sill."

Grandpa and Uncle did not bring water to the animals; the animals went to the water. The corner spring was about one hundred rods from the barn. The hollowed-out log that held the overflow was filled with solid ice on cold mornings. Uncle threw out the chunk of ice and then dipped water from the spring to the log trough. Because Grandfather did not like his cattle to drink very cold water he poured in pails of boiling water to take off the chill.

Sometimes a storm during the night had leveled the road with fresh snow or a high wind had filled it with drifts. Then Uncle had to shovel a path for the animals. The horse was let out of the barn first, and he came a-running. When the snow was soft and wet, his shoes "balled up" and he threw snowballs in all directions. After he had gulped down water he showed off. Sometimes he made a dash up the hill toward McHeard's or rolled in the snow with all four feet in the air. He seemed to roll all the harder when he heard me laugh and shout, "Look, look! Brownie thinks that he is a kitten." When the horse had finished his fun, he went back to the barn. If he met one of the cows on the way, he took pains to crowd her out into the snow. Grandpa used to say, "You notice, Hannah, that Brownie puts on airs. He thinks that he is better than the cows."

The cows did not like the snow and it took some urging to get them to leave the warm barn. Buttercup, in fact, had to be halter-led to the spring. The cows drank silently and rather daintily, not like Brownie who splashed and blew the water.

The oxen, Bright and Star, were the next to come to the spring. They walked gravely, one behind the other, with Star, the nigh-ox, leading the way. Otis, dipping water from spring to trough, encouraged them by shouting, "Gee, Star, gee, Bright; you are good boys." They never splashed the water or crowded each other. Uncle's comment was, "Star and Bright have better manners than Brownie." I was quick to defend the horse. "Yes, but Brownie has a lot more fun."

The sheep were the last to come for water. Usually Grandfather had six, sometimes as many as ten, sheep. Uncle had to fill the trough two or three times before they were satisfied. Grandpa left the door of the sheep pen open and the sheep roamed around the yard for a few hours. Even on the coldest days their gray woolly coats kept them warm.

Uncle Otis's last water chore was to bring two pails of water into the kitchen and set them in the wet sink beside the shed door. We had no well, and depended mainly on the spring for our water. In summer we caught rainwater in the hogsheads that we set under the eaves. In winter we melted snow on the shed stove. Grandma liked to keep the pails in the wet sink water-filled at all times. It was her rule that the stove tank and iron kettle on the stove should be kept filled.

Several times a day Grandmother herself went to the spring. While she worked around the house she kept her eye peeled for an approaching pung or sleigh. When she saw one, she put my outside things on me, threw a shawl over her shoulders and hurried to the corner spring. She always managed to be there filling her pail when the traveler stopped to water his horse. Usually she knew him and called him by name; Captain Chase or Captain Means, Mr. York or Mr. Conary. But whether the traveler was stranger or friend, there was always talk. The depth of the snow, the freezing over of the bay, and the prospect of storm all called for comment. Often there was talk of politics. I always hoped that they would keep off the slavery issue, but they seldom did. When Grandmother began to talk about the wicked slaveowners and to mourn that slavery was spreading into the west, I knew that we were in for a long stay at the spring. When I began to feel cold, I pulled her coat to remind her that I was there. Then she would quickly say good-bye and we would hurry back to the house. For a few minutes Grandmother scolded to herself and then she would say to me, "Hannah, I want you to always hate slavery and to fight it all your life." I did not understand what her talk was all about but I did understand what answer was expected: "Yes, Grandma, I will."

Part of Grandmother's morning work was done in the long, narrow buttery between the kitchen and the corner bedroom. It was here that she strained the milk into yellow earthenware basins. Here she skimmed the cream from the milk that had been setting for twenty-four hours. Here she did her cooking. Her flour board was never put away. It was left on the wide shelf and covered with a piece of old linen. Under the shelf was a barrel of flour and a bag of corn meal. To one side were jugs of molasses, vinegar, and maple syrup; and firkins filled with salt, lard, and coffee beans. Spices were stored in boxes above the flour board. On the wall nearest the window were the coffee grinder and the spice mill. A rectangular maple box divided in the middle held the cooking spoons, knives, and forks. Between the cooking shelf and the window was the dry sink, which was made of wood and had no drain. Grandma took great pains to keep it dry. Its bottom was covered with sawdust and protected by dry newspapers. The dish pan and the rinse pan were always in place in the sink. When Grandmother finished her milk chores and her cooking, she closed the door into the kitchen so that the warm air from the stove would not heat her milk and cream.

I played in the kitchen while my grandmother worked in the buttery. The kitchen was my favorite room. The big iron stove set on the brick hearth. Its pipe went into the great chimney to one side of the brick oven. Behind it was a chimney shelf, very long and very narrow. I could not reach the shelf but I was fascinated by the articles on it. There was a steeple clock, its inside lined with newspapers, its door decorated with purple plums. There was a brown mug filled with loco-foco matches. Beside the mug was a pitcher filled with paper tapers that we used to light the lamps and the candles—that way we saved the matches. On the end of the shelf was a tin tray filled with Mother's and Uncle John Stillman's letters. Grandmother kept them to read and reread. Hanging from hooks on the edge of the shelf was the *Old Farmer's Almanac* and goose wings that were used to brush the stove hearth.

The stoneware dye pot was kept behind the stove. It held about six quarts of fluid, a mixture of indigo, water, and liquid from the chamber pots. The gray homespun dipped into it, wrung out, and dried in the sun became a dull blue. There was a stir-spoon in the pot and I loved to stir the mixture even though it gave out a horrid odor. "Hannah, stay away from that dye pot," was an order that my grandmother repeated and repeated.

The wood box was never forbidden ground for me, though. It stood between the stove and the door that went into my grandparents' bedroom. Uncle filled it every morning before he went to the woods for the day. I hunted in it for pieces of birch. I liked to peel off the bark and decorate it with drawings. If I found gum on the chunks of spruce, I chewed it. I lifted the lighter pieces of wood to the floor and built a fence around my toys. When the box was nearly empty, I played fish pond. I threw metal objects into the box and used a large magnet fastened to a string to get them out. Grandma learned that this game required some supervision from her to keep me from tossing in her thimble and crochet hooks—articles that she thought too choice to be used in a game of woodbox fishing.

Between meals the tip-table became a chair and was pushed against the wall opposite the stove. Two rocking chairs were placed by the west window. Between them was a little stand. During the day it held Grandma's sewing and knitting; in the evening, the lamp and the papers.

After we had had our dinner Grandmother sat in one of the rockers and held me. Sometimes she read one of Mother's letters and talked to me about my mother and father. Often she told me a story about her own childhood when she and Grandma Patience had gone pondlilying in summer and skating in winter on Walker's Pond. Grandma always ended our time of rocking and resting with the same exclamation, "Hannah Wood, this will never do. You and I have chores to do and the supper to start."

The chores were the hen chores. After we had bundled ourselves up we went to the hen pens that stood to the north of the shed. We did not go empty-handed: Grandma carried a measure of corn that had been warming under the stove and a pail of warm water to thaw out the water dishes. The hens were glad of food, but hen-fashion they cackled and flew around and raised a cloud of dust. I was just tall enough to reach the eggs in the lower nests. I took care to leave the wooden eggs that Grandfather had whittled from soft pine. "The nest eggs encourage the hens to lay," said Grandmother. As we gathered the eggs Grandmother encouraged me to count them. I could get as far as twelve. After that she had to take over.

My grandmother always liked to start her supper preparations early. She began by filling the stove box with wood. Then she made two or three trips down cellar. I stood at the head of the stairs and watched her go down. She carried a lighted lamp in winter because snow covered the cellar windows. On her first trip back she brought potatoes, turnips, and apples. These were no surprise to me. She was gone longer the second time and sometimes I would call down, "Grandma, are you there?" She was, and in a few minutes she appeared with a surprise. If I had expected ham or corned beef or hogshead cheese she brought pickled pigs' feet. If I had counted on dried fish or smoked alewives she brought corned mackerel.

She never tried to surprise me about the sweet food. She used to say to me, "There are both gingerbread and applesauce cake in the crock. Get whichever you want." Sometimes she made cup custards or an Indian pudding rich with cream, raisins, and molasses.

While Grandmother started supper, I sat by the west window, rocked my doll, and watched for Grandfather and Uncle to come out of the woods. They came early because they liked to do the barn chores before dark. When I saw them coming, Grandmother helped me on with my outside things and I hurried to meet them. I ran so hard that I often fell in the snow and had to be picked up and brushed off. I was breathless, both from running and talking. There was always so much to tell them: the number of eggs that the hens had laid, that we had gone to the spring twice, that I had lost the scissors in the woodbox, that we were having steamed pudding for supper.

Grandfather and Uncle placed their dinner baskets on the kitchen table, left their axes in the shed, and hurried to the barn to start the chores. Usually the water in the trough had not frozen during the day and so Brownie and the cattle were let out at once for their drinks. But they came out less eagerly than they had in the morning, when they were fed before they were watered. This time things were in reverse order—they were watered before they were fed. After they drank at the trough they trotted back to the barn, intent upon their hay, and in the case of Brownie and the cows, intent upon measures of grain. Uncle and Grandfather removed the manure from stalls and tie-up. Brownie's stall floor was covered with fresh straw. When Grandfather tied a blanket of bags on Brownie, the horse put back his ears in displeasure. Uncle used to say, "Brownie is proud. He would like an imported blanket."

Just as darkness fell, Grandma came to do the milking. I always had our stools in place, hers and mine. I felt that I needed to be there at the milking. I once confided to Uncle, "You know that the cows give down their milk better if I'm there to help Grandma."

After supper was over Uncle shoved the table against the wall, placed the stand in front of the stove, and set chairs around it. While Grandmother did the dishes I sat in Grandfather's lap and listened to him tell about his day in the woods. He told of his walk in the morning: how deep the snow was, that he had seen deer tracks by the brook, and that he had heard woodpeckers working in the poplar grove. He talked about the trees that he and Uncle had cut down; the yellow birch covered with sapsucker holes, the birch with the split top, and the spruces covered with yellow nubs of gum. He gave the details of the nooning: building the brush fire to heat their bucket of tea, placing the birch log for a fireside bench, and warming pie at the edge of the fire. He told me about his walk home, the increasing cold, the waning of the light, and the thickening of the ice on the brook. I liked the way he ended his account, "The best part of the day, Hannah, was having you come to meet us."

Sometimes Uncle rocked me and told me a story. Grandmother called these stories "never-never-yarns." They always started the same way: "Today after dinner when your grandfather was resting by the fire. I walked west on the wood road. Around a corner in the road, whom do you suppose I met?"

This called for guessing on my part: a deer or a bear, a coon or a rabbit, a badger or a skunk. According to Uncle, the animal whom he met talked to him and told him a tale of adventure and danger. The story always ended happily. After I had gone to bed I told it to myself. In the summer when I played at the edge of the woods I was always hopeful that I would see Daniel Deer or Sylvester Skunk or Benjamin Bear. I half expected that they would speak to me.

After I had had my stories the grown people read. My grandparents spent some time with the Bible while Uncle Otis worked on the puzzles in the Almanac. All three looked over the papers, often several days old. When Grandfather and Uncle played checkers, I was expected to be silent. Grandmother knew how to ensure my silence. She broke a feather from the goose wing, handed it to me, and said, "Pretend you are a fly. Flies can't talk." I found this a delightful game. First I tickled Grandfather's neck, then Uncle's, and then the cat's nose. For the sake of my silence Grandfather and Uncle put up with the tickling, but the cat was less cooperative. She jumped from her chair and crawled under the bed, always her refuge in times of trial.

When I started to tire of playing fly, Grandmother brought out an old hand-knit stocking, cut off the worn foot, placed the leg on the knob of a chair, and gave me the end of the yarn. I raveled the stocking and wound the yarn into a ball. I liked to see the leg grow shorter and shorter and the ball grow larger and larger. Quick pulls on the yarn made tiny puffs of dust as the leg was unraveled.

Some part of each evening was spent with work. Grandmother knitted or cut rags for rugs. Grandfather mended harnesses or worked on shoes. Uncle Otis's work was with wood. He whittled spiles or fashioned axe handles. One winter he made butter paddles; another winter, a butter mold with a pattern of four-leaf clovers. The grown-ups included me in their work. I rolled the rags into balls and I swept up the shavings.

While we worked, we talked. I talked about the future, of the spring when Mother and Par Giles would be home, the fall when I would be going to school. The men planned their spring work, speaking of plowing and sowing and clearing land for pasturage. Grandmother wondered where Mother and Uncle John Stillman were. If she sounded worried, Grandfather would say "Louisa, don't worry about where they are now. Be glad that they will be at home soon."

Occasionally we had a caller in the evening. If we looked out the west window and saw a light bobbing along the road, we knew that Mr. Closson was on his way to see us. We put away our work and brushed the hearth and brought extra chairs from the front room. Uncle Zenas seldom came alone. One of his sons, either Joel or Sam, came with him and did most of the talking for his father. There was talk of winter wooding, March lambing, and April tree-tapping. When Joel was his father's companion we had music. Uncle got his fiddle out of the front room closet, tuned it, and played while Joel sang. Most of the tunes were nonsense songs. The only one that I can recall is the one about the weev'ly wheat. It had a great many verses but I remember only two:

> Oh I don't want none o' your weev'ly wheat,
> An' I don't want none o' your barley,
> But I want some flour in half an hour
> To bake a cake for Charley.

> Th' higher up th' cherry tree
> Th' sweeter grows the cherry
> Th' more you hug and kiss a gal
> Th' more she want t' marry.

The Clossons never stayed long enough. We were all sorry to see them light their lantern, put on their coats and caps, and start for home.

Mr. Grindle also sometimes came to see us. He carried no lantern but we knew when he was coming because he shouted off and on all the way from his house to ours. First he called, "Hello the house," and then "Friends, are you at home?" When his calls sounded real near, Uncle opened the front door and shouted to him, "Hello yourself! We are at home. Do come in."

Our neighbor always brought some little gift that his wife had sent to Grandmother and me: cookies or a loaf of bread or a piece of handwork. He also brought some of his own work on which he wanted help. He was attempting to make a basket, something Grandfather made as a young man. Mr. Grindle was eager to learn. He asked Grandfather about shoemaking and iron work and harness making. He queried Grandmother about salting and pickling meat and fish. He stayed a long time and he talked loudly and continuously. Sometimes Grandfather would look at the stirspoon in the dye pot but a sharp look from Grandmother killed his thought of routing our guest by making a stink.

Grandmother always provided a treat for our company. Sometimes she brought out caraway cookies from the buttery. Often she sent

Uncle down cellar for apples or turnips. Apples were passed in a wooden trencher. If turnips were the treat, Grandma pared them and gave each guest a slice and a sharp spoon. We shaved slivers from the slice and savored their cool sweetness.

When Mr. Grindle left for home, Grandmother took pains to send a gift to Mrs. Grindle and to say, "Next time you come, bring your wife with you."

Mr. Grindle was grateful. "Thank you ever and ever so much," he said. He was still saying his thanks when he got to the road. Then he started to shout, "Hello, Belinda! I'm a-coming home!"

No matter how late it was when our company left, Grandfather did not go to bed without going to the barn. When it was very cold or when it was snowing, Grandmother protested against his going but he went just the same. His excuse was, "I sleep better if I know that my creatures are safe and comfortable. Besides, they expect me."

Grandmother's reply was, "Oh, fiddlesticks," but she was always willing to put on my coat and scarf for me so that I could go along with Grandfather.

I liked the squeak of the snow as we walked to the barn. I liked the glimmer of the lantern in the dark. I liked the excitement of opening the barn door and throwing the light of the lantern on the heads of the horse and the cattle. The barn was warm. We could smell the hay and the body odors of the creatures. Brownie whickered a greeting and the cattle rattled their stanchion chains. Grandfather went from crib to crib, from stanchion to stanchion, giving each animal a forkful of hay and calling each by name. After we closed the barn door and placed a prop against it, we looked at the stars. "Hannah, where is the North Star?" asked Grandfather.

I pointed and said, "There it is, right above the corner of the barn."

We looked at the Big Dipper and the Little Dipper. We admired the Milky Way. We waited to see a shooting star. Sometimes we stayed out so long that Grandmother came to the front door and called, "John Friend, bring that child into the house. It is way past her bedtime—and yours too."

Grandma's winter days were not all alike. Wash day was her hardest day—so hard that Uncle Otis stayed at home to help her. She did the washing in the cheese room where there was a small stove. Early on wash day, Uncle built a fire in the stove and set on its top a copper boiler filled with water. The white clothes were submerged in the water and left to boil. Now and then, someone gave the clothes a stir with the clothes stick. Grandmother wore a heavy sweater and a woolen coverall apron while she washed, even though the hot stove and the boiling water took the chill off the room. Two tubs were set on the wash-bench. The hot water from the boiler was poured into the wash tub, fresh water from the spring, into the rinse tub. Grandmother scrubbed the clothes on the scrub board and threw each piece into the rinse tub, where Uncle rinsed the clothing and then wrung the pieces through the wringer.

Grandmother thought that the cheese room was too cold for me so she told me that I must keep house in the kitchen. I was bid to keep away from the stove, to stay away from the buttery and the front room, and keep the door to the cellarway closed. Grandmother sweetened my solitary stay by allowing me to do the dolls' washing. She gave me two milk pans, a bar of soap, and a pitcher of water. My dolls were left naked on the hearth while I washed and rewashed, rinsed and rerinsed their clothing.

It was no wonder that their dresses were so well worn. After the clothes were rinsed, both the family's and the dolls', Grandma and I hung them on the long line that was stretched from the corner of the shed to the sheep pen. I could not reach the line but I did pick up the pins and hand them to my Grandmother. Her rule for hanging out clothes was "to each his own." A hand towel was never caught in company with a dish towel on her line. Grandfather's and Uncle's hand-knit drawers and undershirts were red or blue. Pinned to the line, they soon froze and flapped in the wind like gigantic dried fish.

Grandmother always enjoyed churning. Preparations were made the night before. The up-and-down churn was brought from the cheese room into the kitchen so that it might be at room temperature. The jars of sour cream were taken from the buttery and set on the shelf by the wet sink. The butter mold and the paddles were plunged into a pail of cold water and left to soak. In mid-morning of churning day the cream was poured into the churn and Uncle manned the plunger. As he pulled the plunger up and then pushed it down, we could hear the heavy thud of the cream as it hit the sides of the wooden container. When the butter came, the sound changed to splashing. Then Uncle took the plug out of the bunghole and drained the buttermilk into pails. We drank some of it; Grandmother used it for bread and doughnut mixing, and the surplus was stirred into grain and fed to the hens.

My grandmother took the yellow butter from the churn and rinsed it in very cold water, using the paddles. When all the milk was out of the butter, she took it to the cold buttery, where she worked in the salt and packed the butter into pound squares with each quarter pound section imprinted with a clover. She took great pride in her butter. She put down the extra butter in brine, and sold some of it at the store.

Grandfather built a fire in the brick oven using great chunks of slow-burning apple tree wood. In the morning, after he had removed the embers and the ashes, the oven was ready for use. Grandmother first pushed in a two-quart pot of beans. The beans had soaked all night and were combined in the pot with water, mustard, and molasses, with a generous slab of pork on top. She also baked three loaves of bread in the oven. She had no yeast and made her own rising from salt and hot milk. She also made bonny clabber bread using milk and saleratus. The pies were baked at the mouth of the oven, five or six at a time—enough to last a week. Apple, mince, and pumpkin were our wintertime favorites.

The kitchen stove had an oven that was a foot and half above the stove box and was heated by two pipes filled with hot air. Grandma baked cakes, cookies, and puddings in the stove oven. Twice a week she fried doughnuts in a big iron kettle on top of the stove. The doughnuts were always molasses. White sugar was expensive and so was seldom used for everyday cooking.

Grandmother liked Sunday best. She loved the Lord and she enjoyed going to meeting, but she was not always able to get to church. If Brownie had been hauling wood all the week, Grandfather felt that the horse needed to rest. Sometimes Uncle Zenas or Mr. Grindle would invite Grandmother and me to go with them. Uncle Zenas drove to church in a large, three-seated pung, but even so we were crowded because there were five Closson children. When we went with Mr.

Grindle, we traveled in style. He had a new two-seated sleigh with red cushions and black buffalo robes. Old Gyp, who was not really old, gave us a fast ride to the meeting house. His master made it a noisy one because he was continually interrupting the conversation to shout threats at Gyp. I noticed that he never touched the horse with the whip. When Gyp felt like trotting, he trotted. When he felt like walking, he walked, no matter how loudly his owner shouted, "You lazy bag of bones, get out of your tracks. What do I keep you for anyway?"

The winter of 1851 the ice went out of the bay early and Uncle could row us to church, provided there was a high tide in mid-morning. Had we rowed to the Head-of-the-Bay at low tide, we would have had to walk a long way across the mudflats to reach the shore, something not to be thought of on any day, much less on Sunday.

When we went to church by water, we left the boat at the foot of Christian Hill and walked up the hill to the Baptist Church. It was less stylish than the Congregational Church where the Savages and the Holts and the Darlings went. But I thought that the Baptist Church was beautiful. I loved to look at the carved rose above the front door and the smaller rose carvings above each window. The wooden seats were hard, and Grandmother kept a cushion and a footstool for my comfort. But I was not really thinking of my own comfort. I was admiring the ladies' hats; I was hoping to see children of my age; I was wondering which boy was pumping the organ; I was hoping that we would sing a lot of hymns and that Elder Gilpatrick's sermon would be short. Half of my hopes were fulfilled: we sang five or six hymns; the Elder's sermon was long. But I entertained myself by swinging my legs and thinking about what we would have for dinner. Sometimes I put my head in Grandmother's lap and took a nap.

When we left the church, the Elder always shook my hand and asked me a question. "Hannah," he would say, "What comes after the book of Joel?" I was always able to give the answer because Grandma drilled me every week on the Books of the Bible. He named a different Book every time. I got very tired of his weekly questions and one Sunday, to the distress of my grandmother, I asked HIM a question: "What did Betty Barter do with the bitter butter?"

In winter it was seldom that both Grandfather and Uncle went to church because they felt that it was unwise to leave the fires untended. It was pleasant to have someone at home to start the dinner. Grandma left an easy meal—a pot of beans or a kettle of stew.

When Uncle tended the house, he spent his time with his trumpet, violin, and drum. In the late 1830's when the town had had a militia, he had been the drummer boy. On fair Sundays he liked to pace back and forth between the spring and the barn beating his drum. When he tired of the drum, he blew the trumpet. Sometimes he took his fiddle to the warm barn and played. He said that the creatures enjoyed the music. He told me that Brownie would switch his tail in tune with "The Camptown Races" and I believed him. Sometimes he was so entertained by his music that he forgot to start the dinner.

When Grandpa was the Sunday morning housekeeper, he made an inspection trip of the farm. He went to the hen house and looked over the flock, deciding which were the non-layers that should be killed for the cooking pot. He went to the sheep pen and examined the eyes and ears of the sheep. He looked over the harnesses and the sled chains. Most of his time he spent in the barn. He curried and brushed Brownie and lifted each hoof to see that each shoe was firm. He felt over the oxen and the cows and wiped each with a soft cloth. Grandpa confided to me that he gave the barn creatures a treat on Sundays: scraps of meat for the barn cats; chopped apples and carrots with a sweetening of molasses for the horse, cows, and oxen. I never mentioned this Sunday fare to my grandmother because I knew that she would not approve of Grandfather using her molasses. Every Monday morning she said to me, "Hannah, I wish you could tell me where my molasses goes. I must have used more on Saturday than I realized."

Sunday afternoons we sat in the front room and drew our chairs close to the blazing logs in the fireplace. Grandmother always read aloud from the Bible, especially from the Psalms and Proverbs. Uncle Otis played hymns for the three of them to sing. I did not know all the words but I hummed along anyway. Sometimes Uncle walked to McHeard's to visit with Aunt Abigail Long and her family but he always came back in time to help with the evening chores. While he was away, Grandmother read aloud to Grandfather and me. She considered Children's Bible Stories and The Pilgrim's Progress proper Sunday reading.

We ate our Sunday supper in the front room at the parlor table. Grandma made an occasion of it: she used a linen cloth, her best dishes, and her coin silver spoons. She allowed Grandfather, Uncle, and me to take turns in picking what we would have for supper. My grandfather always chose "pudding"—corn meal mush served with rich milk and sweetened with molasses. Uncle's choice was dumplings with maple syrup. I usually asked for biscuits baked in the Dutch oven, a tin frame that she set close to the roaring flames of the fireplace. She selected the sweet to go with the biscuits—apple butter or stewed fruit or honey in the comb. After supper there was more storytelling and more music and more reading aloud until it was time to make the last trip to the barn and to go to bed.

Every ten days or so Grandfather drove to the Head-of-the-Bay to do some trading. I always wanted to go with him but Grandmother was unwilling. "Your Grandfather has a lot to do, Hannah. You would be in the way and you might get cold. Perhaps you can go next year when you will be a year older." I was disappointed and I could tell that Grandpa was too. He smiled sadly and said, "Your grandmother knows best, Hannah. You be watching for me and I'll bring you something."

Grandfather took eggs and butter to the store and exchanged them for store goods such as molasses and coffee. Sometimes he traded for salt and spices. When the winter pears were yellow and soft, he carried several bushels of them to town. Often he took potatoes and turnips. The village people who had only small gardens began to buy store vegetables by February. Grandfather took with him his red leather billfold that contained a few paper bills and a little silver. But he did not expect to open the billfold. He went to the store to trade, not to buy.

Long before it was time for Grandfather to get home, I sat by the west window and pestered Grandmother with questions: "How much longer will he be away? Is it about time for him?" I pressed my face against the window pane and stared out on the orchard to the road beyond. The tree nearest the window was an old russet whose gnarled apples we seldom gathered. Some were often left on the tree until late winter.

Once, while I waited for Grandfather, a partridge flew into the tree, settled on the lowest limb, and started to peck the apples. I called to my grandmother and she came to stand beside me. I was so excited that I could feel the pulse throb in my neck. I forgot to watch for Grandfather. After the bird finished eating, he perched in the tree looking for all the world like a hen on the roost. "Grandma," I said, "I am going to call him Peter Partridge and after supper I am going to tell Uncle a story about him."

My grandmother replied, "That's a good idea. But I see your grandfather and Brownie coming. Hurry on with your coat and run to meet them." I ran to meet Grandfather, intent on telling him about the bird in the russet tree, but I was not so intent that I forgot to feel in his pockets for the Gibraltars that he always brought me.

Father and Mother Ashore

The spring of 1851 was like the other springs of my childhood. Grandfather and Uncle tapped the maples; they sawed and split the wood; they plowed and harrowed and sowed. Grandmother boiled off the sap; she helped stack the wood; she set hens and geese on clutches of eggs; she cleaned and cooked and sewed. I remember all about these tasks and I also remember the talk about Par Giles and Mother coming home. Mother's March letter told us that they were at Charleston loading with cotton for a Brunswick mill. She wrote, "Expect to see us in May. We have surprising news."

"Surprising news." What could it be? Uncle Otis suggested that Par Giles's brothers had struck gold in California. Grandma felt that the Captain was going to have a larger ship. Once, when my grandparents thought that I was asleep, I heard a conversation that I did not understand:

"Perhaps Eliza is in a family way," said Grandfather.

"Don't you think it," said Grandmother, "Rest assured that Hannah will be your only grandchild. I am sure that Rebecca never intends to provide one."

Expectation of a surprise added to our excitement over the return of the folks. One day in mid-May Grandfather recognized Par Giles's schooner *New York* sailing up the bay before a fair wind. Grandmother had readied the larger upstairs bedroom for my parents but she bustled upstairs to shake up the feather bed and smooth the pillows. She stirred up a gingerbread and cut up Ben Davis apples for sauce. She changed my dress. I could hardly keep still while she brushed and braided my hair. When she finished, I skipped to the barn humming a little song, "Par Giles's on the bay; My Mamma's on the way."

It was decided that Grandmother would keep house while Grandfather, Uncle, and I met the schooner. With the oxen drawing the dump cart, Uncle started first for the town wharf. A little later, Grandfather and I followed driving Brownie hitched to the wagon. We passed Uncle and the oxen near the Doorstone. Brownie was willing to trot. It was as though he sensed our excitement. We were at the wharf before the *New York* got through the narrows.

"Good thing the tide is coming in," said Grandfather. "They'll have no trouble rowing ashore."

As the schooner came into the inner bay, we could see Mother at the bow waving her apron and could make out two sailors shortening the sails. Par Giles was at the wheel. Uncle cupped his hands around his mouth and shouted, "Welcome, welcome home!"

After the sails were lowered and the anchor thrown overboard, a boat was lowered. Into it clambered Par Giles and Mother. The sailors handed down boxes and baskets and bags. "They'll sink the craft if they take any more aboard," said Uncle.

With the gunwales almost level with the water, Par Giles pushed the boat away from the schooner and began to row, first with short, quick pulls and then with slow, wide sweeps of the oars. I lay down on the wharf and leaned over the edge to watch their approach to the landing. Uncle held me by the heels. The tide was far from high; The water lapping the wharf spiles was only two or three feet deep.

"Eliza will have to climb the ladder but she will be equal to it," remarked Grandfather.

We could see that my parents were well tanned. Father's hair was longer than I remembered it and Mother's curls were blowing in the wind. We could hear her say to the Captain, "Faster, row faster—I cannot wait to hold my little girl."

"You'll have to wait until we throw off some of the budgets," said my father.

As soon as the bow of the boat touched the spiles, he rested the oars in the oarlocks and stood up to start throwing packages to Uncle and Grandfather. When the boat was half unloaded, Mother was so impatient that she gathered up her dress skirt and her petticoats, jumped over the side of the boat, waded to the ladder, ran up it, and gathered me into her arms. She seemed so glad to see me that I could not understand why tears were running down her face. In a few minutes Par Giles was on the wharf. He took me from my mother with the order, "Kiss me quick, Hannah!"

We arranged for Grandfather to drive Mother and me to the Corner while Uncle and Father went back to the schooner for firkins and crates. Other belongings were to be brought ashore in the morning.

Mother ordered, "Giles, don't you touch my plants. I want to move my books and my green things myself."

Par Giles laughed when he gave his answer: "That, Eliza, is exactly what I prefer."

Mother's homecoming to the farmhouse was almost as exciting as her wading ashore at the wharf. When we got to our meadow brook, she asked her father to pull up Brownie. "I'm going to run the rest of the way," she said.

She pulled off her slippers and threw them to the bottom of the wagon. Then she jumped over the wheel, gathered her skirts over her arm, and started to run toward the house. The road was dry and her pounding feet made little puffs of dust as she ran. The white heels of her stockings became covered with dirt, her kerchief came unpinned, and the combs fell from her hair. I think that Grandmother must have been looking out the west window because she came rushing out the front door. We watched the two embrace and listened to Mother's laughter. Grandfather did not start up the horses until the women went into the house. Then he clucked to Brownie and said to me, "Your mother, Hannah, always keeps a singing bird in her heart."

Not until the chores were done and the supper was eaten did we hear the "surprising news." After supper, Par Giles pushed back his chair, took me on his lap, and said, "The news is that I'm going to build my own schooner."

Then he told us that last October when he had loaded at Portland with lumber for Charleston, a lumber dealer had offered to help him build a schooner provided that he would agree to take wood products to the Caribbean and bring back sugar and molasses. The deal had been completed in April. Father was to own one third of the schooner; the dealer, one third; and the other third was to be sold to the Captain's relatives and friends. Grandpa and Uncle were quick to offer to buy shares.

"Now the next step is to find a builder," said Father. "I shall go to Verona and Castine and Ellsworth to look around."

"Better go to McHeard's," said Uncle. "I noticed that Joel Long has good timbers on hand."

When the news had been talked over, the presents were handed out. There was a brooch and a length of cloth for Grandmother; a new red pocketbook for Grandfather. When he opened it, he found that it was filled with silver pieces. Uncle Otis's gift was a song book with some music by the new songwriter Stephen Foster. Father gave me a box of paints; Mother, a set of dolls' dishes. By then it was so late that the dishes were done by candlelight. Grandpa had to light the lantern for his bedtime trip to the barn.

The coming of Par Giles and Mother changed the pattern of living at Friend's Corner. There was more in the pantry: my parents had brought firkins of white and brown sugar, bags of prunes and raisins, containers of rice, tin cans filled with bakery crackers and cookies, a jar of curry powder, pounds of nuts, and bottles of flavorings. There was even a bottle of wine. I don't think that Grandma approved of the wine. I noticed that she hid the bottle behind the old teapot on the top shelf.

The house was also less orderly. Mother left books and magazines and tracts on the tables and window sills, and she dropped her knitting work on the floor. Par Giles hung his barometer on the kitchen wall and put his telescope beside the sitting room fireplace. His sailor's bag and ditty box swung from nails in the hall. His sea chest, painted a dull green, stood at the foot of the stairs. Then there were mother's plants, plants that she had brought way from South Carolina. Grandmother never had house plants but she good-naturedly made room for Mother's. The tall oleander stood beside the front door; the azalea, the lavender, and rosemary were each alloted a window sill.

We no longer went to bed at eight o'clock. Every evening Par Giles and Mother told stories about the people whom they had met and the places that they had visited. They had heard Senator Hayne address a political rally and listened to Frederick Douglass when he talked at a Quaker antislavery rally. In Portland they had gone to meet Neal Dow when he opened a Temperance meeting. My father recalled the good sermons that ministers had preached, the fiery speeches that politicians had delivered. He had an eye for fashion and commented upon the newest in waistcoats and cravats. Nor were his eyes blind to the lengthening curls and the enlarging hoop skirts of the ladies.

Mother liked to describe the Charleston mansions set end to the street. But she kept her best descriptions for the gardens. As she talked we could almost see the wisteria and the magnolia, and smell the roses and the honeysuckle. And she told us about southern food; the fried rice, the crabs, the oysters, and the grits. But she was quick to say, "None of it comes up to clams and fish cakes and rhubarb pie." Mother read aloud for a time each evening, sometimes from *Hearth and Home,* sometimes from *Zion's Advocate* and sometimes from a book that she had bought at a city bookshop. When she read from the temperance or antislavery tracts, Father and Uncle were apt to find errands in shed or barn.

My parents took over some of the household tasks. When the Captain was at home, he did some of the cooking. He used sugar and butter and dried fruit with such a lavish hand that Grandma caught her breath. One of his specialties was plum duff—steamed cubes of dried bread combined with raisins and dates and prunes and pieces of apple. We ate it drenched with a hot sauce made of boiling water, brown sugar, flour, and eggs. He made flapjacks, king-sized ones as big as the bottom of the spider in which he fried them. He covered each with sugar and butter and piled one on the other. Then he cut the "jacks" pie-fashion. We had honey or syrup or molasses for topping. When Father made flapjacks for supper, flapjacks were the supper. Sauce was a favorite with father. As long as the Ben Davis apples lasted he made applesauce. When they were gone, he made a rich concoction of dates and figs and prunes. When the berries came, he made sauce from blueberries and strawberries, from huckleberries and dewberries, from raspberries and blackberries, from gooseberries and cranberries.

Grandmother once complained, "Giles, all this sauce making is hard on the white sugar."

He replied, "Louisa, don't you worry about the sugar. I promise to keep the firkins filled." And he did.

I once knew Father to make sauce from dried pumpkin. He sweetened it with molasses and called it "larruping good," but the other members of the family drew the line at stewed pumpkin. Uncle's comment was, "Giles, you'll next be making sauce of burdock and bayberry."

Father did not limit his cooking to sweets, he also prided himself on his biscuits and his dumplings. His chowders and stews were better than Grandmother's because he mixed cream with the milk. (He took pains to do the mixing when Grandma was not looking.) He made meat or chicken pie for our Sunday dinner. The steam vent cut in the upper crust was always in the form of an anchor. When I questioned my father about the cutting in the crust, he said, "The anchor is to show that I started my seafaring days in the schooner's galley. Never forget, Hannah, that you are the daughter of a one-time sea cook."

Father was not interested in planting a garden or in weeding one, but he delighted to pick the produce from one—preferably to give to elderly friends and poor people. No sun was ever too hot to keep him from the blackberry and raspberry thicket. No fog was ever too dense to deter his going to the blueberry patch or huckleberry knoll. He liked to help with the haying and prided himself on mowing more rapidly than did Uncle Otis. He liked to tease his brother-in-law. "Otis," he used to say, "You mow as though you were in the doldrums."

But Father's special farm chore was feeding the creatures. He bought extra grain for them. Soon the hens were having a fourth meal each day. He gave Brownie such full measures of oats that the horse became extra frisky and took up the bad practice of kicking the back wall of his stall. Father also bought himself a horse, a gray and white livery stable horse that he named Whitey in honor of Zachary Taylor's mount of Mexican War fame. Father and Grandfather were Whigs and they felt that it was no mean compliment to honor the president's horse. Like most livery stable horses, Whitey was lean and lank, but with Father's generous feeding he began to fatten up. By August Uncle was saying, "Whitey is as fast as a porpoise."

I once heard Grandfather comment upon Par Giles's liberality, "Giles will never accumulate much in this world. He is too generous with the oats in the horses' feed boxes."

"Yes," agreed Grandmother, "and with the cream in the chowder kettle."

Mother insisted on doing the Monday washing but she did not do it the way Grandmother did. Mother had the men move the wash bench and the tubs and the wringer to the yard beside the shed door. She boiled the clothes and heated the water on the stove in the shed but the scrubbing and the rinsing and the wringing were done in the sunshine. I believe that she liked to wash. She rolled up her dress sleeves, unpinned her dress collar, and pinned back her curls. I believe that she would have sung had she been able to carry a tune. But she did repeat poetry, matching the poems to the rhythm of her work. Her scrubbing was in time to Scott's ballads. "Lochinvar" and "Marmion" got a workout every Monday. The slow beat of "Snow Bound" and "Thanitapsis" seemed right for the less strenuous work of rinsing and wringing. She hung out the clothes in a higgledy-piggledy fashion— shirts rubbing elbows with table napkins and drawers in company with dish towels. She spread some of the washing in the field with the remark, "Clothes dried on the grass will be daisy clean."

Mother offered to milk the cows and make the butter but Grandmother said, "No, Liza, the day may come when you'll have to milk and churn, but not now. You help with the outdoor work and tend your garden."

There was no outdoor work that my mother did not enjoy. She weeded, she stuck the peas, she spread and raked the hay, she made the load, she picked the vegetables, and she dug the first potatoes. She spent hours working in her flower beds that were along the east end of the house. In the beds were Scotch roses, lather-and-shave, London pride, and bouncing Bet, things that lasted from year to year. Then she had hardy herbs like southernwood and dusty miller. She liked to separate her plants. She called it "giving the roots room." She always had a surplus of plants and in June she went "plant peddling." She packed roots and seedlings and slips in a basket and walked to McHeard's or the Doorstone or the old Darling place at the shore.

"You notice," remarked my father, "your mother brings back as much as she takes away." The gift plants were set out in new flower beds dug up on either side of the front door. By August tall hollyhocks were peeping into the parlor windows.

One day when Par Giles had rowed to the Head-of-the-Bay and Uncle and Grandfather were digging potatoes in the back field, Mother said, "This is a good time for me to get acquainted with Whitey."

The horse was in the pasture but she coaxed him to the bars with a measure of oats. While he ate, she put the halter on him. Then she led him to the barnyard where she led him round and round. After a time she removed the long halter rope and tied in two short ropes, one on either side. She threw a blanket over Whitey's back and fastened it with a rope. Whitey put his ears back but Mother quieted him with soft talk. Grandmother had been watching from the kitchen window and she came to the yard to say, "Eliza, I hope that you're not going to get on that horse. You've never ridden, and likely Whitey's never been ridden."

Mother answered, "You are right on the first count but not on the second. The way Whitey moved his back muscles when I tied the blanket on signaled to me that he has been saddled."

Mother continued to lead Whitey around the yard until finally she said, "Both Whitey and I are tired of going round and round. I am going down to Closson's. You two stay here."

We stayed, but Grandma said, "I can tell your mother has something on her mind."

She did. When she got down to Closson's, she had Joel hold Whitey while Sam helped boost her to the horse's back. The next thing Grandma and I knew, Whitey came trotting home with Mother on his back and Sam and Joel running along beside. Mother was jubilant. "See? I told you so," she called, "Whitey is a real riding horse." Mother pulled up the horse long enough for me to be handed up to sit behind her on the blanket. "We are off for the back field," she said, "Come along, Joel and Sam, and you can ride Whitey home from the field."

Par Giles was delighted that his carriage horse was also a saddle horse. He was so pleased that he went right away to Ellsworth and bought a saddle and proper harness. Before the summer was over both he and my mother were good riders. Mother made herself a skirt split up the front so that when she rode her legs and ankles were covered. "It would never do to shock the village ladies," she said.

Mother made changes in the routine of my life. I no longer slept in the trundle bed in my grandmother's room. Mother insisted that I have a room of my own. I was given the small corner bedroom back of the parlor. The large spool bed nearly filled the room. Grandma put a bright hooked rug on the floor and spread on the bed a blue and white coverlet that Grandma Patience had made. For a night or two my mother slept with me. I felt secure with her arm around me. She told me stories until I went to sleep. After a few days I consented to sleep alone. I took pride in referring to my "parlor bedroom," and I liked to make my own bed and dust the candle stand beside it.

Mother decided that I should improve my knitting by knitting every day. She took up some stitches on big needles and gave the instructions, "Now you are to do a stint every day—ten rows. I'll leave the needles and yarn on the parlor table. I shall look every evening to see if you have done your stint."

Doing my knitting proved to be no problem at all—Grandma did it for me. Some days Uncle Otis also knit a few rows. Mother was delighted with the firmness of the stitches. She exclaimed with pleasure when twenty rows had been added to the work. She never suspected that I was being helped, but Par Giles did. When Mother praised me, he used to laugh and say, "It appears that you have a knitting prodigy in the family, Liza. Perhaps a double one."

All winter my grandmother had kept me close to her. Only when I went with Uncle or Grandfather was I out of her sight. Mother changed that. I heard her tell my grandmother, "I want Hannah to go about the farm alone. She must learn to look after herself."

One day Mother suggested that I walk to Closson's to play with little Kate, and I started off feeling grown-up and well pleased with myself. At the little bridge over the brook I stopped to watch the flow of the water. It was quiet. I could hear the splash of the water against a boulder and the "teacher-teacher-teacher" of an ovenbird. Suddenly there was a sharp cry in the bushes beyond the brook—likely a fisher or a marten. I turned and ran back to the kitchen where Grandma was stirring up bread. I hid my face in her apron and cried. Mother pulled me away, dried my tears, and said, "Why don't I go to Uncle Zenas's with you?"

At the brook Mother and I stopped and she talked to me: "You are not frightened when Brownie whickers, or when Buttercup moos, or when the pig grunts. Wild animals don't whicker or moo or grunt. They have their own sounds. You must learn that sounds cannot harm you."

Every day after that my mother encouraged me to go off by myself. When I came back to the house, she asked the same question: "What wild creature did you hear talking today?"

I was pleased when I could report, "I heard a fox bark," or "I listened to two hedgehogs squabbling over drops under a wild apple tree."

With Par Giles and Mother at home we had more company. There was a difference between callers and company. Callers were those who dropped in without an invitation. Company were folks who had an invitation and for whom a special treat or meal was prepared. Of course the same people could be both callers and company. When Mr. Grindle came to borrow a tool or ask advice, he was a caller; when he and Mrs. Grindle were bid to tea, they were company.

Sometimes we asked the Means, Saunders, and Closson children in for the evening. Mother played with us. She helped Abbey and Kate and me to find hiding places when we played hide-and-seek. She was the judge when we played tag and tug-of-war. But when we had races, she ran. Joel and Sam did not like it much when she outran them. Father stayed in the kitchen and made the treat—corn balls or molasses candy or soft gingerbread. Once, he fried flapjacks for us. He spread each with molasses, then we rolled them up and ate them with our fingers. When we had finished, we raced to the brook to wash our sticky hands.

Sometimes Mr. and Mrs. Closson, the Grindles, and Captain Means and his wife were asked in for the evening. Then there was sure to be music, and dancing too. Otis played the violin for the folks to sing. Without music Par Giles and Captain Means sang sea chanteys. Mother could not sing but she loved to dance. At that time a lot of people frowned upon dancing. When Mother and Father came home from the voyage, Mother told how she and the Captain had learned to dance while they were in the South. "Would you mind if we danced in the parlor?" she asked.

Grandpa was so slow to answer that Grandma had to pony him up. "Come, come, John, do speak up. Of course we don't mind. Whatever you want, Eliza, we want."

Grandfather nodded and said, "Louisa and I might help to make up a set if we are not too tired."

I was allowed to stay up to watch the folks dance. Par Giles did the calling and Otis played the fiddle. Now and then Otis danced and Father played a jig. He played by ear and he made more sound than melody. Before the summer was over, Mr. Grindle learned to call the directions and he delighted to do so. Otis's comment was, "Milford calls so loud that he keeps Daisy and Buttercup, Brownie and Whitey from their rest." I always fell asleep while the dancing was at its height. Grandma undressed me and put me to bed.

So I missed the treat. Mother, however, always saved something for me. I had it for breakfast with a cup of warm milk. The evening treat included tea or coffee. Usually they had cakes. Father made two to make sure there would be a-plenty. Sometimes he made what he called "Cuban Cake." It was made from brown sugar and filled with soft, purple raisins. Apricot-nut was a loaf cake that he baked in a long bread tin. Occasionally he made cakes in layers and piled them high with whipped cream. Grandma was never pleased to have the cream used for cakes. She wanted to sour it and use it in the churn. In August Par Giles baked "grunts." These were deep-dish pies filled with blueberries or cherries or raspberries. Once he used huckleberries—but only once. Uncle's comment was, "Huckleberries are good in a rhyme but not in a pie." Then he would sing,

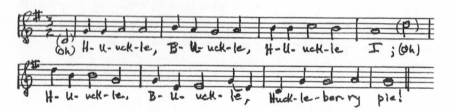

I think he used a hymn tune, for I noticed that Grandma shook her head over the huckleberry song.

Sometimes our guests were asked for supper or for Sunday dinner. Aunt Abigail and her family were often invited. Father and Mother liked to entertain Father's first mate, Jairus Osgood and his wife, Elizabeth, Captain Melatiah Chase and his wife Eliza. Then we ate in the parlor and used the gold-banded dishes and the best silver and linen. My grandparents liked the excitement of having company. Father did the cooking for guests but Grandma washed up after the meal. She could trust no one but herself to handle the good dishes.

Callers and company did not quite satisfy Father's desire for sociability, though. He suggested that we have Wednesday night prayer meetings in the school house. When he brought up the plan, there were objections.

"But who will preach?" asked Mother.

"I shall," he replied.

"People will be too tired to come," said Grandfather.

"It will rest tired people to talk with the Lord," countered my father.

"There won't be enough people to have a meeting," objected Uncle.

"Enough if we ask the people at the Doorstone and McHeard's," replied Father.

Par Giles went ahead with his plans. During July and August he held meetings every other week in the school house. Otis and Joel Closson gave duets, we all sang hymns, and my father preached. A few people testified. Mr. Closson's testimony was always the same. He thanked the Lord that he had learned to live with his cross. Mr. Grindle's was the shortest and loudest. He gave thanks for his prosperity. When Mr. Long came, he asked God's forgiveness for his habit of exaggeration. He ended his plea with the confession, "Lord, I have shed barrels and barrels of tears over this fault."

After the service the congregation was invited to our house. The men sat in the backyard and the women gathered by the front door. The children were all over the place. Par Giles and Uncle busied themselves passing out the treats. We often had switchel in big white cups. This was really a haying-time drink made from molasses, nutmeg, ginger and cold spring water. Par Giles always made molasses bars but he varied them by using a different dried fruit—raisins or apricots or dates. Once I heard him suggest to Grandma that he make sour cream cookies. She soon vetoed that suggestion.

The use of cream was not the only matter over which Par Giles and Grandma did not see eye to eye. They disagreed over the extension of slavery. Grandma's family had belonged to the American Colonization Society, which hoped to free the slaves and send them to Africa. Pushed by Parson Fisher of the Congregational Church and by the Bangor Theological Seminary, it was real strong in this area. Grandma herself was a member of the Antislavery Society and read the "Belfast Republican," a weekly that condemned slavery and slave owners. Grandma's estimate of slavery was, "sin"; of slave owners, "sinners." Par Giles had met slave owners, and had in fact done business with them. He could not see that they were any different from northern businessmen. He knew that a big cotton crop meant good times for New England mill owners and shippers. I once heard him say, "Cotton is the thread that holds the Whig party together."

When Par Giles and Grandma discussed slavery, the other grownups left the room but I stayed. I liked an argument even though I knew how it would end. Said my grandmother, "I'm sorry, Giles, to see you take such a weak stand against the spread of slavery. If you read the 'Belfast Republican' your views would be sounder."

He replied, "I do read the 'Republican' and that is why my views are what they are. I regard that paper as rabid and fanatical."

"When you are dealing with evil, it is a virtue to be a fanatic," triumphed Grandmother.

Then there was the matter of the schooner cat. The cat had come aboard at Charleston and been named Pickens by the Captain, who ordered the cook to feed the cat the best food in the galley. Father said that the cat earned his board by catching all the rats aboard ship. When Par Giles handed over the *New York* to the Ellsworth owners, he brought Pickens ashore. The cat adjusted well to farm life. He continued his aggressive campaign against rats and his devotion to the Captain. He moused in the meadow, caught minnows in the brook, and slept in the haymow. But he chased the barn cats, Jed and Joe, out of the barn and terrorized Grandma's pet, Tiger, so that he hesitated to go outdoors. The only creature that put Pickens in his place was the old gray gander.

Finally my mother put her foot down; "Giles, my mother and father will never complain but I am sure that they feel badly at the way your cat abuses theirs. You'll have to put your cat away. Tiger and the barn cats were here before Pickens came."

Father let his chin drop—a habit that he had when he was distressed. "But Eliza," he said, "you know I do not like to kill any creature."

"This time you will have to do what you don't like," said my mother.

Several days went by before the matter was again brought up. Then Mother declared, "If you don't kill Pickens today, I'll have Otis shoot him."

This time Par Giles replied, "I'll kill him if you'll let me select the method of execution."

Mother said, "Fair enough, shoot him or drown him. It makes no difference to me." Then she hurried back to the kitchen and we heard her slam the back door.

I stayed with my father and burst into tears. "I don't want Pickens killed," I wailed.

"Now don't take on," said my father. "You leave everything to me and Pickens will live out his nine lives."

I was told to find the cat and fetch him to the orchard. When I returned with the captive Pickens in my arms, Father had moved an old table under the limb of a cherry tree to which he had tied a short rope. He lifted Pickens to the table and tied the rope around his neck. He talked soothingly to the cat and reassured me, "Everything will come out all right, Hannah. Just wait until your mother comes out into her flower garden."

In a few minutes we heard the side door slam. When Mother took in the scene under the cherry tree, she ran screaming to the orchard, "The idea of hanging a cat! Giles Wood, cut Pickens down at once. You are a cruel, unfeeling man to do such a thing in front of your little girl. I'm mortified, I'm ashamed, I'm mad clear through!" Then she stamped her foot and started to bawl.

Father looked sheepish and said, "Eliza, I was only doing what you ordered me to do. You agreed that I could use any method of killing that I wished."

He smiled while he removed the rope from Pickens's neck.

Mother dried her eyes. "Captain," she declared, "you are a cunning man, I don't believe that you intended to kill the cat at all."

The subject of all the contention jumped down from the table, stretched, and padded off into the thick grass.

That afternoon Mother and I went to the back field to pick strawberries. When we got home, I heard Grandmother say to my mother, "Giles drove to the Head-of-the-Bay this afternoon. He had Pickens with him—tied up in an old bag. I expect that he dropped him into Peters's Brook."

"I expect so too," said my mother.

I had no such expectation but I kept quiet.

For the next few days Pickens's name was not mentioned. Joe and Jed returned to the barn and Tiger was once again the king of the cat kingdom.

A few weeks later when we drove to church, Mother asked Father to haul up the horse in front of Jairus Osgood's. "I want to admire Elizabeth's white roses behind her iron fence," she said.

I noticed that father hesitated but after a minute he did halt Whitey and we saw the white roses. But the roses were not all we saw. On the top step of the front door rock there lay Pickens napping in the sun.

Mother exclaimed, "I can't believe my eyes. Is that Pickens?"

Said the Captain, "You had better believe them. That is indeed Pickens. He has transferred his affections from the Captain to the First Mate and has a new port of call."

Journeys With the Captain

"**G**et Hannah into her best gear," were Par Giles's directions to my mother when I went to Bucksport with him. My "best" was a long calico dress with a beruffled hem. Father wore a silk vest, a black taffeta cravat, and a suit he had bought in Boston. When we were ready to leave, Grandmother and Mother looked us over. Mother said that we looked like city folks and Grandmother warned that our good clothes would be dust-covered when we got home. Father refused Grandmother's offer of a tin of breakfast biscuits for our lunch. He helped me into the buggy, picked up Whitey's reins, and said to Mother, who had followed us to the yard, "Well, Liza, the wind seems to be fair. I guess we'll cast off."

Bucksport, a Penobscot River town some eighteen miles from Friend's Corner, was the home of shipbuilders. Father was going there to talk with the owner of an Orphan Island yard.

The road from Grandpa's farm to the Head-of-the-Bay was familiar to me. I kept up a chatter of talk about the families whose homes we passed. I am sure that my father's mind was on the business ahead but he kept nodding his head and saying, "Yes, yes, is that so?" while I talked of Mr. Grindle and Uncle Zenas and Abbey Saunders and the Whitneys.

After we left the village we changed roles. Father became the talker and I the listener. I gave close attention to all that he told me. He pointed out the haze atop the mountain and prophesied, "It will burn off and be hot today."

Beyond the mountain we passed a field where there was a cellar hole with lilacs around it. "A farmhouse once stood there," said Father. "It caught afire, and it was a good thing that it did. The fire got a woman out of bed who had been there for three years. A very foolish woman, if I do say so. She was the youngest daughter of the farmer who lived here. She thought that she was in love with a neighbor's son. When he went off and married a girl from Sedgwick, she declared that her heart was broken and she went to bed. She might not ever have gotten out of bed had the cat not upset the lamp on the kitchen table."

"What did the cat do then?" I asked. I was more interested in the cat than in the lovelorn maiden.

"The cat did plenty," answered my father. "The overturned lamp set afire the cloth on the table and the fur on the cat's back. The terrified creature rushed to the haymow and in minutes the barn was all ablaze!"

I had sorrowful thoughts about the cat but Father's narrative had returned to the bedridden girl. "She jumped right out of bed, grabbed a quilt, rushed down stairs to the kitchen and beat out the flames. After the fire was out, she went back upstairs and dressed. Folks said that she never again mentioned her broken heart. A few years later the house was struck by lightning and burned. The family moved to a better farm on Calf Town Ridge and the girl married a rich widower."

I could tell that my father thought this story had a happy ending. I didn't, so I made up a better one. I imagined that the cat had fled to the bedroom where the girl had rescued him before using her firefighting skill in the kitchen.

Father's tale about the fire whetted my appetite for more stories. At each house that we passed I asked, "What happened here, Par Giles?" Usually his answer was, "Nothing much, Hannah. The folks lived happily ever after."

But in front of a large clapboard house well shaded by elms he pulled Whitey to a stop and said, "Now something really important happened here. Once there was a time in Blue Hill when everyone belonged to the Congregational Church and the town collected a tax to support the church. In your Grandmother's silver luster pitcher are the receipts for Grandsir' Friend's church taxes that he paid the town. About 1806 some of the members left the church and formed the Baptist Church—my father was among the come-outers. But the town continued to collect money from the Baptists for the support of the first church and its pastor, Parson Fisher. Even the Baptist minister was expected to pay. After a time the Baptists protested against paying the tax. When their minister refused to pay, the collector seized his cow. Then the Baptists were really mad!

"The man who lived in this fine house was a red-hot Baptist and he declared, 'I shall never again pay the church tax and if the collector comes to take my cow there will be trouble.'

"The collector *did* come; there was trouble. He came the day the farmer was mowing out the orchard. With swining scythe, he drove the collector off the premises. He took one swipe at the man's ankles—just enough to bring the blood.

"This incident is what old folks used to call 'the church war.' It set people to thinking, and at the next town meeting the Baptists were excused from paying a church tax to the town."

Father finished his story and clucked to Whitey to start. I thought over the story and asked the question: "Did Grandpa Friend ever chase the tax collector?"

My father laughed when he answered, "Hannah, you know the answer. Your grandfather is too gentle to chase anyone. Now Grandma Louisa is different. I can imagine her chasing someone with a scythe."

"Not with a scythe," I corrected, "with a butter paddle."

At a long rambling farmhouse my father remarked, "They say that a man was once murdered here."

"Do tell me all about it!" I urged. My grandparents had with care shielded me from the sights and sounds and words of violence. I was exiled from the barnyard when Uncle Otis killed a hen. Grandmother skipped the Bible stories about the sacrificial lambs and Isaac on the altar. As a result I hungered for tales of catastrophe and bloodshed.

"Well," said my father, "this is the way I heard the story. I don't vouch for it. Years ago a tin-pedlar was seen walking into the dooryard here at suppertime. He had a sack of his wares swinging from his shoulder. He was never seen again alive. The next day his body was found on a rock about two miles from here—now called Dead Man's Rock. His sack was hanging over an alder bush but it was empty. The man at this house was questioned and he insisted that the pedlar had left for Bucksport after supper. The strange thing was that for decades that household had plenty of tinware—spoons and pans, dippers and pails—and yet a tin-pedlar was never seen to come to that house."

Near the Blue Hill-Penobscot line we passed a new house on the left. It was unpainted and the chimney untopped. Father looked at it and said with regret, "I wish that we had time to stop here. I'd like to see Lighthouse-keeper Clay."

When Father was silent, I interrupted his thoughts with the query, "But where is the lighthouse, Papa?"

My father laughed, "It is not here, Hannah. Mr. Clay once kept the light off Little Deer Isle. Many times at night I've seen the glow of the light and by day have waved at the keeper. They say that Mr. Clay loved the sounding of the fog bell and the pounding of the waves in a storm. But after his little girl died during a spell of bad weather when the sea was so high that he could not go for the doctor, he brought his family ashore. I suspect that he thinks every day of the island and the light and the ships that sail up and down the Thoroughfare."

After we crossed into the town of Penobscot, Father pointed out Dead Man's Rock to me. At my request Father stopped Whitey and I was allowed to get out of the buggy and stand on the flat, moss covered rock. I thought of its desirability as a playhouse and said to my father, "I wish we had a Dead Man's Rock at the Corner."

When we reached the height of land in North Penobscot, Father stopped to rest Whitey and to dip a bucket of water for the horse from the barrel-spring. I got out of the buggy and picked a few strawberries that were reddening near the spring. We turned to look southeast and saw the Mount Desert hills in the distance. To the southwest was Blue Hill Mountain, a clearer blue than the distant range. Father said, "If we could only stand atop the North Penobscot Church we could see Castine and the Penobscot River to the west."

Orland was the next town. Before we entered the village at the foot of a long, twisting hill, we made another stop where Father turned teacher. He taught me that Orland was once called "Oarland" and that it is located on the Narramissic River. He pointed to the hills to the northeast and said, "Those are the Moose Horn Hills of East Bucksport, where Abbey Saunders's father lived."

It was dinner time when we got to Bucksport. Father drove to Jed Prouty's Tavern that overlooked the river. A boy met us at the steps and after we had alighted, he led Whitey to the stable back of the inn. When my father guided me into the dining room, I understood why he had told Mother to have me wear my best dress. There were half a dozen tables in the room, covered with linen cloths and set with sparkling dishes and glass and shining silver. And there was a waitress. I had never before eaten in a hotel and was too bashful to answer when she asked, "Will you have beef or lamb?"

Father answered for me, "I'm sure that Hannah's choice is lamb. Please put a lot of gravy on her potato."

When it was time for dessert, I was silent when the waitress asked, "Custard or rhubarb pie?" Again my father spoke up, "Bring her some of both."

After Father paid for our dinners at the desk, the clerk invited us to sign in the tavern's register. In a bold hand Father wrote, "Captain Giles J. Wood." Under his signature I printed "Hannah L. Wood." Then the clerk proudly flipped back the pages to show us the names of General Winfield Scott, General Zachary Taylor, Martin Van Buren, and Daniel Webster. As we went down the tavern's steps, Father said, "Hannah, today we have dined in style."

My reply was, "I hope that Whitey dined, too."

We left the horse at the livery stable and walked to nearby Orphan's Island, which was connected to Bucksport village by a footbridge. We went to the home of the boatbuilder, where I stayed with the builder's wife while he and father went down to the ways. The builder had made trips to China and had brought back a collection of little bells. The bells were on a small octagonal table in the parlor. I was invited to play with them. My hostess and I spent a happy afternoon. She sewed seams; I rang bells. When the men returned from the yard, the woman hurried to meet them and whispered a few words to her husband. He was a big, gruff man with large feet and hands. He picked up a little brass bell, rang it, and handed it to me and said, "This is a bell from a Chinese temple. I'd like you to have it. Take it home with you."

My delight overcame my shyness. "Thank you, thank you ever and ever and ever so much. I'll keep it always. I'll put it beside my little purple shell."

"That, too, came from the Orient," my father hastened to explain.

On the way home both Father and I were silent. He was considering business terms, I was busy ringing my bell and thinking about far-away China. I rang the bell until I fell asleep. The next thing I knew we were driving into the home yard.

After the family had eaten supper, Par Giles told about our upcountry ride. He described the blue sky and the green meadows and the view of the Mount Desert hills. He commented upon our journey pauses and our tavern dinner. He outlined his business talk and praised the builder and his wife for their kindness to me.

When Father had finished, my mother asked, "What did you like best about your trip, Hannah? Was it picking strawberries or eating a tavern dinner or ringing temple bells?"

My mother and my grandmother were confoundered by my answer: "Standing on Dead Man's Rock."

Father's next trip was to Ellsworth. For a time I feared that I would not be allowed to go with him. I could tell that Grandmother regarded Ellsworth as a very wicked city. She said, "The ways are all on Water Street. That used to be called Rum Row. There's no knowing what kind of people you'll see there: likely, a lot of those wild Irish from the Old Country who have come here to work in the sawmills."

Father smiled but said nothing. On the morning he proposed to go to Ellsworth, he swept aside all of my grandmother's objections, "Rum is no longer sold legally in Ellsworth. The Irish from the Old Country are little different from the Yankees of this country. And Hannah will be safe with both Otis and me to look after her."

Grandmother was reassured when she learned that Uncle Otis was going. Father pleased her by asking for a tin of breakfast biscuits. "This time," he said, "we'll have a bite in the carriage before we cross the river into the city. It will be cheaper than eating at the Hancock House. Hannah need not wear her best dress."

At Grandfather's suggestion, Brownie was used for the twelve mile journey to the shire town of the county. Uncle Otis drove. I sat between my uncle and my father and held the whip, an article that was for show and not for use. We went by way of McHeard's, where we stopped briefly at Aunt Abigail's brick house to leave a basket of currants that Grandmother had picked for the Longs.

The six miles from McHeard's to Surry, the next town, were all uphill, down dale with the road twisting and turning. At Morgan's Corner where there was a stand of young oaks, the road made a sharp left-hand turn. There Uncle Otis pulled up the horse for a rest in the shade. I scrambled out of the carriage to pick up last year's acorns, softened and faded from a winter under the snow.

In Surry Village we crossed a plank bridge where the boards clattered and rattled when Brownie trotted over them. Near a large brook was a small store where strings of smoked fish swung from a line tied between two trees. Uncle Otis's comment was, "What a mess of smoked alewives they have for sale. On the way back I'll buy a string for Louisa. She loves them."

"Don't buy a string for Giles," said my father. "When I eat fish, I want flesh, not bones."

It was late forenoon when we neared Ellsworth. We paused at a roadside spring to let Brownie drink and crop the roadside grass while we ate biscuits and doughnuts that we washed down with spring water. While we rested, Father told me, "In a few minutes we shall pass the Black Mansion on our left. I want you to look sharp at it. It was built by Colonel Black, who came here from England as a timber agent. He became rich and he knew the famous men of his day. His brick house looks like the plantation homes that your mother and I often see in South Carolina."

When we drove past the mansion, I exclaimed over it because I could see that Father expected me to admire it. But I was more impressed by the wooden, four-story Hancock House which stood on the west side of Union River. We crossed the bridge into the city and looked up Main Street where the brick shops were built wall-to-wall. Father pointed to the granite block buildings and the granite window sills and foundation stones of the brick buildings. "All the granite came from Blue Hill," he bragged.

We turned sharp right and went down Water Street, which followed the river. Here were wooden stores on the left; on the right were sawmills and boat shops built high over the steep river banks. We heard the raucous sound of saws and smelled the resinous odor of newly sawed boards. There were few people in sight. I asked Father, "Where are the wild Irish from the Old Country, Par Giles?"

My father gave me a lesson in understanding: "Now Hannah, just forget what your grandmother said. The Woods and the Friends once came from Old England. We are now Americans. The Irish came more recently from Old Ireland but now that they live and work here, they also are Americans."

When we came to a long shop with the swinging sign, "NAHUM HALL SHIPBUILDER," Father said, "This is the man I want to see. Notice that he has two schooners on the ways. One is for Samuel Morrill, a master whom I know real well. We'll hitch Brownie in the shade. Otis, you and Hannah do the sights of Main Street while I talk with Mr. Hall."

Before we left, Father gave me a dime with the injunction, "Now Hannah, keep this in your pocket. If you lose it, I shall not give you another."

As my uncle and I walked up Main Street I grasped his hand with one of mine. In my other hand I held the dime. We walked along the plank sidewalk and looked in the shop windows. There was a jewelry shop with watches and combs and toys in the window, then a stationer's store where the windows were filled with books. There were numerous grocery stores. The two apothecary shops had identical window displays—mortars with pestles and glass jars filled with pills. Another shop window was filled with pictures of men, women, and children. "The man who runs this shop," explained Uncle, "is called a Daguerrean artist. I expect that some day he will take your picture."

"But not today," I said. "I don't have on my best dress."

Just as I spoke, I opened my hand. Down dropped my dime and disappeared down a crack in the sidewalk. The crack was too narrow for Uncle to get his fingers down; nor could he reach under the walk. I began to cry and lament, "Par Giles said he would not give me another if I lost this one. And I was going to buy lozenges to take home to Mother, Grandma, and Grandpa."

Now dry your eyes," Uncle directed. "If you play your cards right you can get another dime from your father."

I was given careful directions. An hour or so later when my father appeared, I rushed up to him with the query, "Par Giles, is a dime lost when you know where it is?"

His quick answer was, "Of course not, Hannah."

I said, "Then I have not lost the dime. I know where it is. But will you please give me another?"

Uncle and I pointed to the dime under the walk. Father ruefully laughed and shook his head but he handed me a dime. "Hannah," he said, "You had the advice of a smart lawyer. Let's hurry into Means's Store so that you can spend this dime before you lose it."

The three of us went into the general store. I invested my ten cents in candy selected from the assortment of Gibraltars, jawbreakers, lozenges, and peppermints. Father bought presents for those at home: tea for Grandmother, candied ginger for Grandfather, and a comb for Mother.

Uncle Otis bought a harmonica that he played all the way home. He played folk tunes and Father hummed along with him. He played hymns and Father sang the words. By the time we reached McHeard's Uncle had run out of tunes and hymns. Then father made a suggestion, "Otis, I'll sing you a sea chantey. Then you pick up the tune and play it on the harmonica."

I couldn't sing then any better than I can now but I did learn some of the words. I still recall these four lines that give directions about handling sails in a blow:

> First the rain and then the wind
> Topsail sheets and halyards mind;
> First the wind and then the rain,
> H'ist your topsails up again.

Building the *Meridian*

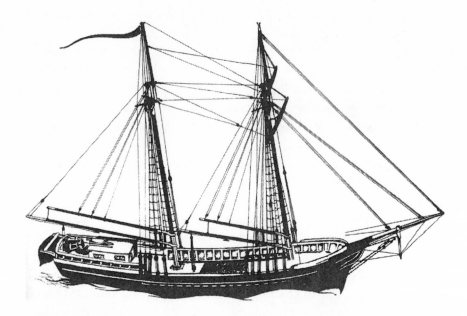

As it turned out, the schooner was built not on Orphan's Island, not in Ellsworth, but on the Mill Stream Cove at McHeard's. The builder was Joel Long. He got the job because his prices were lower than those of out-of-town builders. Having the schooner built in town meant that my father could go every day to the ways to check on the progress of the work. Sometimes he took a hand in the building. Uncle Otis, when the farm work let up, turned carpenter for a day or two. I often went to the cove with Father.

The ways had been built on the east side of the cove. First, the men pounded two rows of logs in the ground parallel to the field that edged the shore. The tops of the logs were smoothed and pine boards were nailed to them, forming a track that sloped to the shore where it passed through boxes that had been filled with stone and earth. The ways started so near the bridge that when the schooner neared completion, its bowsprit stretched above the bridge. Teams had to drive under the sprit. Some of the horses did not like having the timber above their heads, and they shied.

First, the keel of the schooner was laid and then the frame, with sternpost, stern, bow cants, and bilge stringers, was nailed in place. Once the skeleton was built, work shifted to the outside of the craft where planking was fastened by trunnels and caulking daubed between the cracks.

While Par Giles talked with Uncle Joel or worked on the schooner, I had the company of Clara Long, a child a year younger than I. She was the daughter of Uncle Joel and Aunt Abigail. Sarah Miller also tagged along with us. Her father was Captain John Miller, who had built a handsome clapboard house overlooking the boatyard. Daily we three made the circuit of the yard and watched the men at work.

Near the road were piles of logs that had been twitched out of the woods the preceding winter. We liked to sit on the logs with our dolls. We imagined that the piles were schooners and that we were bound for faraway places like Port-au-Prince and San Francisco and Canton. In the meadow near the ways were several buildings; a shed open at one end where the men could work in wet weather, a carpenter's shop, and a steam building that held a huge iron stove. On the stove were two large iron kettles filled with water. The water was kept boiling when the schooner was being planked. Some of the planks had to be bent in order to be fitted over the frame, and only a plank softened by steam could be curved into place. Clara's brothers, George and Moses, had charge of the steaming process. When Sarah, Clara, and I heard the boys call, "Hot plank, ho," we ran to the steam shop and followed the hot plank from steam box to boatside.

The blacksmith shop was on the west side of the cove at the foot of Hyer's Hill. My playmates and I loved to go into it to feel the heat from the forge and to watch the sparks that flew from the hot iron as it was struck by the heavy hammers. One day a spark landed on my doll's dress and set it afire. Quick as a wink the smith doused the doll into the hogshead of water that stood near his forge.

Not far from the smith's shop was a sawpit. It was a hole dug deep in the ground, perhaps thirty feet long and four feet wide with ways and rolls across the top. When a pit was in use, a stick of timber was placed on the rollers. One workman stood above the stick; a second worked in the pit. The two of them pulled a whipsaw that trimmed timbers and sawed them into planks and boards. The man in the pit covered a portion of his face with a handkerchief to keep the sawdust out of eyes.

We little girls liked to lie at the edge of the pit and watch the men at work. The sight of the man with a partly covered face amused us and it was not long before we were laughing at him and calling him "Handkerchief Harry."

The sawyer was not amused. One day he said, "If you young ones do not stop laughing at me, I shall jump out of the pit, catch you, and throw you into the pit where you will smother in the sawdust."

We did not heed the worker's warning. One day he did indeed jump out of the pit and started to chase us. The three of us started running to the steam shop. I was the slowest runner and so I was the one that the sawyer caught. He held me under his arm and ran back toward the pit. I struggled against his body; the smell of sweat on his dirty shirt made me sick. My heart pounded and my head reeled with dizziness. I was silent in my terror.

But Clara and Sarah were not silent. Their screams brought my father and Uncle Joel running from the carpenter's shop and summoned Aunt Abigail with flour-covered hands from her kitchen. Red-faced, the sawyer dropped me. I did not hear what Father said to him because Aunt Abigail herded us back to the kitchen. Hot cookies and mugs of cold milk made me forget my run-in with Harry. However, I never forgot the lesson I learned: it is both unkind and dangerous to make fun of a person.

Father and I always brought a lunch of biscuits and doughnuts which we ate in the coolness of the carpenter's shop. If we looked out the open door, we could see the blue bay with the Mount Desert hills beyond. If we looked through the opposite window, we saw the Mill Stream with Uncle Joel's gristmill and sawmill.

While we ate and rested, Father told me about his plans for the schooner. He intended to take on some ballast for the trip to Portland but hoped for at least a partial cargo of bricks, cordwood, and ventures. He explained that ventures were items that people entrusted to the captain to sell for them. "For instance," he said, "Uncle Zenas plans to have several bushels of turnips to send and your grandmother is making cheeses, some ten pounders and some twenty pounders. I expect to drive to North Blue Hill to see if some of the farmers there have potatoes and apples that they would like to have me sell for them."

Father went on to tell me what he would do in Portland; "There we'll throw out the ballast and unload the bricks, wood, and ventures to sell to local dealers."

I knew that the Cuba-bound cargo was to be shooks, staves, and long lumber, and that the cargo out of Cuba would be sugar and molasses.

Father commented that the market for molasses in Portland was not as good as it once was; "Since the legislature passed 'the Maine Law' it is not legal to sell liquor in the state—nor is it legal to make it. Portland once ranked second to Boston as the biggest rum making city in the nation. Years ago, when we sailed into Portland harbor we could smell the malty odor of the great vats."

"But where do people now get their rum?" I asked.

My father laughed ruefully and replied, "I hope that they are getting less. Now liquor is illegally brought in from other states; some is made at home. But whoever has rum on hand, whether innkeeper or houseowner, takes care to hide it. Sheriffs and their deputies are always on the look-out for hidden lots of bottled drink."

The naming of the new schooner was often talked about in the Friend household. Grandpa hoped that the craft would be called the *Louisa and Eliza*. Mother suggested the name *Hannah and Florence*. Grandma thought up such romantic names as *the Curling Wave* and *the White Foam*. Uncle Otis had fun thinking up ridiculous names. My father laughed as heartily as anyone over the names *Wood's Wagon* and *Giles's Galleon*. My father suggested no names and warned us, "Remember that Mr. Jackson in Portland has advanced the most money for the schooner and so it is his privilege, if he wishes, to name her."

It was a privilege that the Portland man exercised. A few weeks later a letter came from Portland. It announced that the schooner would be called the *Meridian*.

Grandma and Mother were disappointed, but the menfolks approved. "The name has a musical sound," said Uncle Otis, and to prove it he sang,

Grandpa said, "I like the sound of the word. Does it have something to do with midday?"

"Yes," replied my father," and it also means a circle that is used in reckoning longitude. The schooner has a good nautical name. May it be a sign that she will always have safe sailing."

Some days Father did not go to the ways. He did errands for the schooner. The smith at the yard did not make the heavy ironwork and so my father engaged James Clough and his son James Russell to make the chains and the anchor. The Cloughs lived to the west of the Head-of-the-Bay. The elder Clough was a great joker. Father used to say, "I like to go to see shipsmith Clough. He can joke even about a funeral. At the time of the drowning of his brother-in-law he said, 'A death in the family has its favorable features, as it prompts a relative to buy a new suit of clothes to wear to the funeral.'"

Father and Mother drove to Castine to make arrangements for the purchase and the later delivery of sails and ropes. Because they went on a schoolday I did not go, and was disappointed. I wished very much to visit a rope-walk and a sail loft. My father knew that I was sad about missing the trip to Castine so he brought me a very special present—a little model of a schooner. It had two masts all rigged with sails.

After supper Par Giles sat the model on the kitchen table and taught me the names of the sails on each mast; (on the foremast, the foresail, the fore gaff-topsail and the square sail; on the mainmast, the mainsail and the main gaff-topsail.) He taught me that the triangular sail carried at the bow is the jib. Nearly every evening he had a review of the sails and taught me sea terms. By late October when the schooner was ready for launching, I talked of hawsehole, bilge, martingale, scuppers, and bulwarks like an old sailor.

When mother noticed how quickly I learned, she took a hand in my nautical education. To Captain Wood's delight I learned to repeat the thirty-two points used in boxing the compass, complete from "nothe" to "nothe-by-west." My mother taught me a verse about night navigation:

> When both lights you see ahead,
> Port your helm and show your red.
> Green to green or red to red,
> Perfect safety—go ahead.

On Saturday, Par Giles took me with him when he went to call on Jairus Osgood and to see a farmer at North Blue Hill, a section that folks called "the dark of the town" because it was back of the mountain and so got less morning sunshine.

Father had asked Mr. Osgood to go as first mate on the voyage to Cuba. Mother did not approve of the choice. She said to Father, "You know that you and Jairus never hitch horses. I'm fearful lest you have a collision in midstream."

"Liza," said Father, "Make up your mind to use either barnyard or aboard-ship metaphor. Jairus and I rub each other the wrong way but we do respect each other. He is a fine sailor."

The afternoon that we called on the Osgoods there was no sign of disagreement between Captain Giles and First Mate Jairus. We found Mr. Osgood in his barn admiring his new sea chest, one with metal corners and handles—a far better one than my father's, which had old rope handles. The Osgood chest was painted blue with its owner's name in black letters painted on the side. Mr. Osgood had a family of seven little boys. He and his wife Elizabeth made no secret of their desire for a daughter. He gathered me into his arms with exclamations about my curls and blue eyes. He delighted me by setting me in the sea chest.

Soon Elizabeth Osgood came across the road from the house. She had a baby in her arms and a little boy tagging at her heels. After she had talked with the men I went back toward the house with her and we lingered in the yard. She proudly pointed to the new iron fence that bordered two sides of the yard and connected with a picket fence that ran along the south and the west sides of the yard. She left the baby in a cradle set in the sun while she showed me her garden; the hollyhocks growing behind the iron fence, the white and red currant bushes by the picket fence, the patch of mustard greens by the barn, and the hop vine that spilled over the north side of the fence. There were three apple trees and three plum trees growing in the yard. Little Thomas Osgood listened to his mother with rapt attention as though this were his first trip in the yard. He was silent until we came to a bunch of burdock. Then he found his tongue: "I hate burdock. When I have a cold, Ma wraps my feet in the leaves and then ties Pa's stockings on my feet. Gee, don't my toes itch!"

"Yes, I know," said Thomas's mother, "But the leaves draw the cold out of your head."

Mrs. Osgood left Thomas and me with the bidding, "Now you two play nicely together. I must take the baby into the house for his nap."

We might have played nicely together had not Pickens, the cat, who had been asleep in the burdock patch, appeared upon the scene. I recognized him as an old friend and rushed to gather him into my arms.

Thomas misunderstood my gesture. "You can't take Pickens home with you. He is now our cat. Captain Wood gave him to us."

My reply was aggressive: "I guess I can so take him home if I want to. What Par Giles gave away, he can take back if he wants to. Pickens is going back to Grandpa's."

Thomas took no chances on losing the cat. He seized Pickens by his hind legs while I pulled on his front legs.

The cat made it clear that he was Pickens's cat. Quick as a flash he scratched my arm. When I dropped his forequarters, he turned and bit Thomas's arm. Then he retreated in high dudgeon to the burdock patch. Thomas' screams had greater volume than mine but mine were higher pitched. Mrs. Osgood rushed from the house to comfort us and to lead us to the kitchen for drinks of cold milk.

The men in the barn must have heard our outcry although they did not intervene. After our visit was over and my father and I were in the carriage ready to leave for North Blue Hill, Mr. Osgood made a remark that set Father to laughing: "We'd better take Hannah and Thomas to sea with us. In a fog mull, their screams would carry further than the sounding of bells and horns."

After my run-in with Thomas I was relieved that the North Blue Hill farmer whom we visited had no sons. He and his little girl, Tillie, met us in the yard; we fastened Whitey to the hitching post, and went into the long, low barn whose shingles were gray with age. Along one side of the barn were barrels, some filled with potatoes and some with apples. The men walked from barrel to barrel commenting upon the size and the quality of the vegetables and fruit. Father took a Bellflower from a barrel, pared it, quartered it, and ate it with satisfaction while he and Tillie's father talked prices.

Tillie led me to a large barrel in a dark corner. The barrel was topped with a ragged quilt and on it lay a money cat with her family of four black and white kittens. Tillie and I stood on a box to reach the kittens and I shouted to my father, "Come quick, Par Giles, and help me pick out a kitten to take home."

There was quick reaction from the men.

Said the farmer, "Children, come away from that barrel right now."

Said my father, "No, Hannah. You can not take a kitten home. Your grandmother has all the cats that she wants."

We obeyed and left the dark corner but every few minutes we went back to cuddle the kittens. When the old cat jumped down, we covered the kittens with the quilt.

"Tillie," shouted the farmer, "You girls go and play outside in the sunshine."

It was not long before the traders came from the barn. Father lifted me into the buggy, unhitched Whitey, climbed into the buggy, and with whip and reins in hand prepared for a dignified departure.

His final words were "I'll get word to you when you are to deliver the apples and the potatoes at the town wharf—eighteen barrels."

Then I felt that it was my turn to take part in the business negotiations. I turned to Father and in a voice loud and clear asked, "Aren't you going to buy the kitty barrel? That has bottles in it—full bottles. I saw them when we covered the kittens with the quilt."

Father did not speak; he acted. He gave Whitey a sharp cut with the whip. Our departure was rapid and rakish.

Whitey was unused to the whip. He showed his indignation by giving us a swift trip back to the Corner. We were home before my grandmother expected us. She bustled to the barn to inquire, "Did everything go alright?"

"Just fine," answered my father, "but your granddaughter created incidents when she sought to repossess Pickens and advised me to purchase a barrel of contraband liquor."

Mother had chores to do in preparation for her voyage on the *Meridian*. She asked Grandfather and Uncle to set Par Giles's sea chest in the sun. She washed the interior with suds and water and then scoured it with a square of sandstone. Next she gave the outside a coat of green paint. She and Uncle Otis had some words over the color that she selected.

"You ought to paint the chest blue, Liza," said Uncle Otis, "Blue for the ocean."

"That shows how little you know about the ocean," replied Mother. "Deep water appears to be green to a man aboard ship. Besides blue is the color of farm carts and wagons."

Uncle Otis, a farmer at heart, was quick to answer what he regarded as a slight to farming: "I'll have you know that a blue cart is worth as much as a green chest—worth more, for a chest is hard to move, not like carts and wagons which are blessed with wheels."

My mother had the last word when she quoted the old saying: "Who wouldn't sell a farm and go to sea?"

She left the packing of the sea chest to the Captain but she filled her own chest, a small box that Grandfather had built for her from pumpkin pine grown and cut on the back lot. In it she packed several sets of steel knitting needles and a supply of yarn. Grandfather's sheep had furnished the wool; Grandma had spun the yarn; Mother dyed the yarn using dyes made from acorns and black-eyed susans. She put in her sketch book and a new box of paints with fresh brushes. The box was topped with empty scrapbooks, her Bible and Fox's Book of Martyrs and Pilgrim's Progress. She promised herself that when she got to Portland, she would buy some books for the voyage.

"No use to buy the books in Ellsworth," she said, "If I did, I'd read them right away. I can no more let a book alone than can a drunkard, a jug of rum."

My mother had Uncle Otis help her tie up bundles of "Zion's Advocates" and the "Belfast Journals." On the trip she cut up the papers to get materials for the scrapbooks.

"I don't know why you make more scrapbooks," complained Uncle. "The house is full of them now."

Mother used a higgledy-piggledy method in pasting in her clippings. A sermon by Henry Ward Beecher often had to share a page with a cake recipe. A poem rubbed elbows with a rule for filling the dye pot. Antislavery pronouncements, riddles, short stories, editorials, political platforms and puns; they were all in the scrapbooks.

Grandma urged Mother to take a supply of medicines with her. My mother demurred: "You know that I am never sick, Mother. Giles and his crew are all young and right in the pink."

She finally consented to take a bottle of hens' grease, a can of camphor, and pieces of flannel. This pacified my grandmother. "At least you'll be able to treat folks if they have bad colds," she said.

Mother felt sorry that she could not take her plants to sea. In August she began to dry leaves of Sweet Mary and fragrant-leaved geraniums and sprigs of southernwood and thyme. When they were dried, she tied them into a bag made of old linen. "There," she said, "I'll take this bag aboard ship to remind me of the fragrances of my garden."

Some of Mother's chores were for the benefit of those who stayed at home. At her suggestion, Grandfather closed up the parlor fireplace to accommodate a Franklin stove that Father bought in Ellsworth.

"Now you can use this room when it is cold," she said. "Some of the heat will warm Hannah's little bedroom."

She laughed when Uncle Otis accused her of buying the stove to protect her house plants: "Now you can sail away carefree, Sister, knowing that the oleander and the Boston fern will not be frostnipped come December."

Mother bought for me a map of the eastern coast and the Caribbean Sea. It was uncolored, and she spent a number of afternoons painting it, giving each of the fourteen Atlantic seacoast states a different color. This required a lot of paint-mixing. I recall her comments about her color choices for two of the states: "Maine's color will be green for her forests. I'll paint Florida brown for its swamp water and snakes."

With a fine pen she made dots on the map to show the location for Blue Hill, Ellsworth, Portland, and Havana; then she printed the names on the map.

She said to me, "You look at the map, Hannah. That will be a good way for you to learn geography. A better way would be for you to come with us, but not this time because now you have to start school."

The launching of the schooner was set for October 30th, a day when high tide came at two o'clock. Before the launching there was much to be done at the yard. Grandpa and Uncle slighted the farm work to help with the last preparations. Melted pitch was spread over the oakum that had been forced into the seams on the schooner. The hull had to be painted. The top of the ways and the bottom of the slides were greased with a horrid mixture of soft soap and beef tallow with a sprinkling of flaxseed to help hold the grease on the wood.

Mother and Grandmother were as busy as were the men. For a number of days, they baked tin after tin of hard gingerbread. I watched them mix the bread so many times that to this day I know the rule for hard gingerbread. Here it is:

1/2 cup of molasses
2/3 cup of shortening
1 heaping teaspoon of soda
1 cup of hot water
1 tablespoon of vinegar
Ginger to taste
Enough flour to make a soft dough

I remember that they dissolved the soda in the hot water. After the ingredients were put together, the mixture was kneaded and rolled out in thin sheets. The bread was baked in what Grandma called "a moderate oven."

I never liked this gingerbread very much. It was not sweet enough to please me, but it was good for outdoor eating because it did not crumble.

The day of the 30th dawned cool and clear. All of us were up before four o'clock. It was still dark when Father left for the yard. The rest of us left later, after all the chores were done. For once the house was deserted. In fact, the entire neighborhood was deserted because the Grindles and the Clossons and the Saunders family all went to the launching. Mother and Grandma drove Whitey. I went with Uncle Otis in the ox cart drawn by oxen borrowed from Mr. Grindle. In the cart we had tubs of gingerbread, a gallon of cream, a gallon of long-sweetening, and tins of coffee. Old mugs and cups borrowed from the neighbors were piled in a wash boiler. Uncle took along both his drum and trumpet.

The oxen made a slow trip to McHeard's. When we reached the top of Hyer's Hill, we stopped to rest the creatures and to admire the schooner on the ways. Using words that I had heard from my father, I spoke up, "She is a 130-ton craft. I can tell by her looks that she will be weatherly, a good sailer, and a fair carrier. She is no appletree-er. She'll sail deep waters with safety."

When we reached the cove, we found that all was confusion. Moses and George were rushing to tend the fires in the steam house stoves. Grandma was tending the coffee. Mother and Aunt Abigail were setting up sawhorse-plank tables in the orchard. Father and Uncle Joel and Mr. Osgood were inspecting, testing, and planning.

Finally Par Giles shouted, "All hands off the vessel. Stay on the west side of the cove and keep back from the water's edge. Please be quiet so that you can hear the sound of the mauls on the blocks and the splash of the schooner when she slides into the water."

We were silent; we watched; we waited. Workers went under the bottom of the schooner, and going from stern to bow in pairs, with a man on each side, they split out the blocks on which the keel rested.

Soon there was a creak and the sound of falling timbers. The men jumped for safety.

The *Meridian* moved slowly at first; then she gathered speed and slid swiftly and safely into the water. Once she was afloat, there were cheers from the onlookers and loud beating of the drum and blowing of the trumpet. The children and the womenfolks had been so excited watching the launching that they had forgotten my father's warning to keep back from the water's edge. When the schooner hit the water, it made a wave that wet their feet and skirts. It knocked over little Sarah Miller, whose screams almost drowned out the drum and the trumpet. Her father dealt with her by giving her a gentle spank with the admonition, "Always remember that a captain's daughter never bawls at a launching."

My father was pleased with the launching. That evening he explained that it was considered bad luck to have a schooner stick on the ways at the launching. "The *Meridian* came down the ways clean, swift, and clear," he bragged. He also explained why the masts were not stepped until after the craft was in the water; "The height and weight of the masts might interfere with the balance of the schooner as she slides down the ways."

Father expressed his pleasure with the name of the schooner; "I am glad that the schooner has a nautical name. There is an old idea that it is bad luck to name a craft for living persons. It is likely only superstition but all the same…. And it is no doubt bad luck to have a woman on the ship when she goes down the ways."

My mother laughed and remarked, "I notice, Giles, that you don't think it bad luck to have a woman aboard when a vessel goes to sea."

It was some days before the schooner was ready to sail. After the masts were stepped, the rigging had to be set up and the sails bent on. Par Giles and Mr. Osgood did the work but they called upon Captain Candage to help. Captain Candage had "swallowed the anchor" when he married the widow Walker, whose first husband had been lost at sea. She had insisted that her second husband give up being a sailor. It was a strange thing, but it seems that Phoebe Walker Candage had a premonition that the sea was to take her loved ones. All of her seven sons went to sea and five of the seven died in foreign ports or were lost at sea.

Father did not hurry about the work with the sails and the ropes. He did not wish to put to sea until the hurricane season was over because he took great stock in the old saying

June, too soon;
July, stand by;
September, remember;
October, all over.

He planned to make two trips to the Caribbean before late May when the malaria season made it wise to give up going to the islands. During the summer he would go coasting, taking Ellsworth lumber or Penobscot bricks or Castine rope and fish to Boston or New York or Charleston.

Once the *Meridian* was under sail, the Captain with his crew of Mr. Osgood, Mr. Harding, and Moses Long (who went along as cook) sailed the vessel to the town wharf at the Head-of-the-Bay. My mother went with them, for as she said, she wanted "to get the feel of the schooner." She wished me to go with her but I had a ready excuse, "We might be late in getting home and I have to be here to help Grandma with the milking."

I could see that Mother was disappointed and that Grandmother was pleased. My grandfather did not say anything, but after my uncle and mother left for McHeard's Cove, he called me to his shop and gave me a square of maple sugar.

"Why, Grandpa," I exclaimed, "I thought that the maple sugar was all gone."

"Not quite," he said. "I kept back a little for a special occasion."

At the time I thought that the "special occasion" was the launching of the *Meridian*. Now I know that it was something very different.

I had no regrets about staying home. The day that the Cuba-bound *Meridian* sailed for Portland, Uncle Otis drove my father and mother to the landing but I chose to remain at the Corner. My father estimated three o'clock as the hour for sailing and so soon after four o'clock my grandparents and I walked down the steep hill to Porgy Point where we stood on the ledges to watch the schooner sail down the bay. When she was opposite us, Mr. Harding rang the ship's bell and the other men swung their hats while Mother waved her big white apron. I jumped up and down on the rocks and Grandpa threw his hat into the air.

When the *Meridian* passed between Long Island and the Sand Point and entered the outer bay, my grandparents and I turned from the sight of the sea and started to walk up the hill.

I walked ahead of the others and sang a little song: "Shan't go to Havana, Havana. Happy to stay at the Corna."

Flavilla

Before Mother and Par Giles set sail on the maiden trip of the *Meridian,* they arranged that Grandma's grandniece Flavilla Billings would come from Brooksville to spend a month with me. That was in 1851, the year that I became seven in mid-November. I had not met Flavilla but Mother had told me all about her. "She's ten years old and a big girl for her age. I can tell you that she has learned to look out for herself. She can outrun her brothers, ride a horse, tread a load of hay. She is a merry girl, always laughing and talking. You'll miss your father and me less with Flavilla here to keep you company."

I looked forward to Flavilla's coming. We expected that her grandfather, Grandma Louisa's brother, would drive to Friend's Corner and spend the night before returning to the Walker Pond neighborhood where he lived. Every afternoon I perched on the peaked rock between the barn and the spring and looked up the road in hope of seeing the Brooksville company drive in sight.

I never did greet Flavilla. It was Flavilla who greeted me. She came to the Corner not by buggy but by boat. On a Tuesday when there was a stiff west breeze blowing, her uncle brought her over in his pinky. They surprised the Friends by walking into the kitchen just as they sat down to dinner. After a quick meal, the uncle sailed home. Because I was at school, I did not see Flavilla's uncle or the pinky. (It was years before I learned that the craft was not painted pink.) So Flavilla had all the afternoon to get acquainted with the family. When I came home from school, she was sitting on the peaked rock waiting for me.

When she saw me coming she ran to meet me, her ruffled skirt bobbing like a blue balloon. Her flat straw hat blew off into a clump of frost flowers. Her long straight hair blew straight behind her. When she reached me, she bent to kiss me and to take my slate and dinner pail. Then she began to talk, and she did not stop until we walked into the kitchen.

"Ever since Uncle went home, I've been thinking about names. Names are very important, I believe. Your name has been a puzzler. I have a Cousin Hannah at home. Of course I call her Hannah. You are my second Hannah and so I shall call you Hannah-Hannah. I've decided to call your grandfather and grandmother Uncle Grandfather and Aunt Grandmother. Your Uncle Otis is my cousin and I shall call him Cousin Uncle. I hope that you don't know another Flavilla. It would be awkward for you to have to call me Flavilla-Flavilla."

Flavilla had to stop to catch her breath when we went into the kitchen. After I kissed my grandmother and showed her my letters on the slate, Flavilla and I went into my corner bedroom, where she pointed out to me how she had stowed away her belongings. Three calico dresses hung from a nail on the back of the bedroom door. Small piles of petticoats, drawers, and handkerchiefs were in the corners of the top drawer. Nighties and knit stockings were in the second drawer. "I may be here until the snow flies," she declared. "I hope that I stay ever and ever so long, maybe until Christmas."

Our guest showed no sign of homesickness. When it was time for Grandma to milk the cows, Flavilla offered to get the supper. "Just tell me what you plan to have and I'll get it," she said. "I can make biscuits and flap-jacks. You should see the pile of jacks that my brothers can eat. And it takes about a quart of maple syrup to float the flap-jacks." After supper she insisted on doing the dishes alone. "That's the way I do the dishes at home. I work best in single harness. Don't worry, Aunt Grandma, I shall not nick the dishes."

There was daylight left after the work was done up. I suggested that Flavilla and I walk to the brook. When we got there, we hopped from plank to plank of the bridge. Then we leaned against the top bar of the railing and I told Flavilla about Mother and Par Giles and the *Meridian* and the trip to the Caribbean. When I finished, she confided to me that she expected to be a sea captain's wife.

"The Tapleys are just about the best-known family in Brooksville," she said. "There are seven sons and every one of them is a sea captain.

Of course I cannot marry one of them. They are all married and besides, they are older than I. But they have sons and I intend to marry one of them and go to sea. There is a woman in Penobscot, who went to Australia when she was about my age. A captain asked her to go on the voyage as company for his wife. He told her that if she would go he would have the ship's carpenter make her a china cupboard. She went and she got her cupboard. I've seen it. I went to her house once with my father. The cupboard is just beautiful. It has a glass door; there is a mirror between the top of the drawers and the shelves. On the shelves are white ware dishes. I shall have such a cupboard someday and I'll fill it with English china—maybe pink luster."

The splash of a fish breaking water in the brook turned our thoughts from imported dishes to running water.

"Too bad it is too cold to go wading," I said.

"Well, it's not too cold to rail-walk," declared Flavilla. "Now, Hannah-Hannah, I am going to dare Flavilla to walk the railing."

I was quick to offer objections: "Grandma won't like it."

"She won't know about it," countered Flavilla.

I came back with another objection, "You'll fall off into the brook and get wet."

"No, if I topple, I'll fall on the plank side," was her quick reply.

"Then you'd get splinters in your hands," I said.

"What if I do? Splinters pull out," replied Flavilla as she took off her shoes, jumped lightly to the railing, pulled up her skirt, and walked the rail without incident.

I was filled with admiration and rushed to hand her her shoes. She brushed off my cries of praise; "Oh, don't make such a fuss. I am always daring Flavilla to do something. But I make sure that I can do it before I throw down the dare."

In the following weeks Flavilla dared herself to walk a high beam in the barn, to slide down the henhouse roof, to ride Par Giles's Whitey bareback, and to go from the spring to the brook in a series of cartwheels. She never dared me to participate. Only once did a dare get Flavilla into trouble.

One day after school, she and I sat on the peaked rock and ate apples. We threw the cores to the young stock grazing in the open barnyard. When we had had our fill of windfalls, we sat and watched the three fat heifers. Suddenly Flavilla said, "I dare you, Flavilla, to catch the black-and-white heifer by the tail."

Before I had time to protest, she ran to the unsuspecting creature and seized her by the tail. Action was instantaneous. The heifer uttered a blat of alarm, kicked up her heels, and dashed about the yard as though pursued by a demon. Flavilla's feet were now on the ground and now in the air but she did not loose her grip. My cries of alarm brought Grandma from the kitchen and Grandpa from his shop. Words never came quickly to Grandpa, and he was speechless. Not so Grandma; "Leave go of that tail at once! The creature is crazed. You will be lamed for life. I say let go!"

Flavilla did let go, but not because of Grandmother's bidding. Her skirt ruffle was her undoing. The ruffle was ripped and she caught her foot in it. She fell, and out went her hands to cushion her fall. By that time Uncle Otis had come from the barn. He picked up Flavilla, brushed her off, and said to the winded heifer-catcher, "Cousin, you are always talking about being a captain's wife and sailing the Seven Seas. I think it more likely that you will be a circus performer and join Barnum and Bailey's."

Flavilla soon recovered from her bruises. Even this incident did not cure her of "daring Flavilla." My grandfather allowed that the heifer never recovered. She grew into a large and handsome cow, the best milker in the herd, but she would never let a woman or girl get near her. Uncle Otis had to milk her. When girls or women went to pick plums in the pasture, she betook herself to the middle of a thicket.

Flavilla made the Friend homestead a lively place and she also brought liveliness to the one room school opposite Uncle Zenas's. The first morning that she went to school, the Corner scholars stared at her long hair and commented on it. "I won't have it pulled," she said. When someone commented on the length of her legs, she retorted, "The better to catch you with when we play tag." When Albert Whitney called her an "out-of-towner," she said, "I'm an 'in-towner' in Brooksville the home of the famous seven Tapley brothers, all of whom are sea captains. I'll bet that Blue Hill does not have seven seafaring brothers who are captains."

Blue Hill didn't. The best that we could do was to mention the seven Candage brothers who went to sea. Under her questioning we had to admit that only two of them were captains. At that, she brushed aside the Candage claim to maritime fame.

The leader in our neighborhood school had always been Joel Closson, whose good natured father allowed the pupils to get water from his well, to gather apples from his orchard and to lunch on the "stripped fish" hanging in an out house. Joel was as good natured as his father. He was the best reader in the school; he spoke clearly and loudly; even the five syllable words did not get his goose. His tenor was pure and true. He decided what games the boys would play at recess time and at noontime. It was he who settled the playground quarrels.

Flavilla's coming to District Seven gave a jolt to Joel's leadership. When we opened school with the singing of "America," her full alto drowned out his tenor. When the teacher tested her reading, he placed her in the class with the twelve year olds—Joel, Willy Means, and Relief Whitney. At noontime, the girls as usual retreated to the grove to eat dinner and to play games. The boys ate in the schoolyard and then played ball there. It had always been customary for the girls and the boys to play separately. That was a custom Flavilla did not like. "This is no fun here," she said. "Let's go to the road by the big rock and I'll teach you a game that we play all the time at home."

The game was "tap-on-the-back-run-a-mile." It involved roughness, running, and loud shouting. The master came to the door to watch and laugh. The boys stopped playing ball, and in a few minutes, uninvited, joined the girls in playing the new game. "Tap-on-the-back" was not the only game that Flavilla introduced to the Corner children. Within a week, Joel was saying to her, "What shall we play this noon, Villa?"

Joel's sharing of his schoolhouse honors—musical, scholastic, and playtime—brought him the favor of the girls of the school. The Means and Whitney Sisters were always saying, "We wish our brothers were like Joel."

One night Flavilla confided to me, "I may not marry a Tapley after all. I might marry someone from Blue Hill, provided of course that he went to sea. I just have to have some way to get to California."

Our Brooksville visitor went home in early November. We did miss her. My life was less exciting. Grandma missed her help in the kitchen. She was often mentioned. Grandpa talked of her high spirits and Uncle was always saying, "I wonder what Flavilla dared herself to do today?"

When Flavilla returned for a late May visit, we learned all about her winter doings: and how she had slid down Kenches' Mountain on a Cape Racer, how she had skated on Walker's Pond when the ice was cracking, how she had made sourdough bread when her mother was away, how she had cleaned out the tie-up all alone the day that her father and brothers had attended town meeting, how she tapped maple trees and boiled off the syrup. She described the launching of Captain Robert Tapley's schooner, the *Mark Potter*. She told us about going to Castine where she saw kiln-wooders loaded with wood for the Rockport and Rockland kilns.

Flavilla was welcomed back to the homestead and the schoolyard. But her chief adventure of the spring was not in the barnyard or the schoolhouse. It was in the town of Sorrento, and it was an adventure shared by Uncle Otis and by Aunt Abigail Long, Clara and me. It was also shared by Grandpa's Brownie.

Grandfather Friend was one of twelve children. Eunice was one of the youngest, and she had married Bradford Brown of Sorrento. Grandpa always looked sad when anyone mentioned Eunice Brown. Grandma did not look sad—she looked provoked, and she scolded, "I have little patience with Eunice. When she found that she had married a blunderer, she should have taken over the bossing of the farm; she is capable. But as it is, she just puts on a long face and bawls when Bradford gets into a scrape. And what scrapes he has! Burning down the smokehouse, getting the oxen mired in the mud, leaving the potatoes in the ground until they froze, running the sink drain into the well. I have no patience with Bradford, none at all."

Grandpa dropped his chin and looked very sober as he always did when Grandma criticized his relatives.

In a few days we heard more about the Browns. One night after supper we had a call from Aunt Abigail and her youngest child, Clara. When I suggested that Clara and I play in the dooryard, my cousin refused; "Oh, no. We want to stay right in the kitchen and hear what my mother has come to say. I wish that she would let me tell it. I can talk lots faster than she can." Clara knew her own talents. Her speech was speedy and effortless.

Aunt Abigail slowly and with some repetition told that she had heard that Bradford's mother had died. Finally she came to the point of her visit, "I feel that some of us should go to the funeral. It's tomorrow. Now that Eunice has trouble, she will need someone from her own family with her. I think I should go. I'd like to go and take Clara. She has never been to a funeral and this seems like a good chance to break her in. The catch is that Joel can not go 'cause he's all tied up with Captain Cousins' schooner. What had I better do, Brother?"

Grandfather was so slow in answering his sister's plea that Grandma prompted him, "Come, come, John, speak up or else Abigail will think that you do not wish to help her."

Grandfather finally made the suggestion that Otis take Brownie and drive Clara and her mother to the funeral.

Clara gave it away that her father and mother had discussed this plan. With a rush of words, she hurried to say, "My father is willing for Otis to take our double-seater. That way Flavilla and Hannah can go. We'll have to take a picnic lunch and eat on the way. We'll have mourning caps and have lots of fun."

It was Grandmother who stopped Clara's burst of enthusiasm; "Clara, a funeral is no time for having fun. I am willing that Flavilla and Hannah should go with you, provided of course that Otis can take a day off from the planting. Flavilla may go to the funeral; she is going on eleven. But Hannah is only seven. She will have to stay outside. She is too young to view a corpse."

My regret at being excluded from the funeral rites was softened when I learned that I was to have a mourning bonnet. After Clara and her mother left for home, I was sent to summon Belinda Grindle to help Grandma make bonnets for Flavilla and me. The women pulled apart an old bonnet of Grandma's that she had worn at the funerals of her parents. Using the material from the old bonnet, after much cutting and hemming and trying-on, they turned out two bonnets. Flavilla's had a flat top on which was perched a rosette of dull black net. Mine had a peaked top crested with a velvet bow. Both tied under our chins with lutestrings. We were so excited over our bonnets that we hated to take them off and go to bed.

We got an early start the next morning. Flavilla and I wore our best gowns to pay honor to the occasion and to equal the style of our bonnets. Uncle wore his Sunday jacket with a black ribbon tied in the lapel. He had fastened a black ribbon in Brownie's right blinder. My grandparents saw us off. Grandma pushed a firkin filled with biscuits and seed cakes under the buggy seat. Grandpa said, "We'll expect you back by dark."

At the Long's we left our carriage and hitched Brownie into Uncle Joel's two-seater. Young George had washed it and his mother had tipped the whip with a black ribbon. Aunt Abigail got into the front seat with Uncle. She wore a black gown with a black-and-white cameo at her throat. Her huge beveiled hat bespoke the prosperity of her mill-owner, shipbuilder husband. Clara sat in back with Flavilla and me. She wore a mourning bonnet topped with a black peony.

As we drove from McHeard's to Ellsworth, there was little talking. Flavilla was less lively than usual and Clara's flow of conversation was slowed. Whenever we started to talk, we were sure to meet a team. The driver would haul up and ask, "Where's the funeral, folks?"

The answer was always the same, "At Sorrento. Bradford Brown's mother is dead. We are Mrs. Brown's relatives."

We were asked the question so many times that we finally took turns giving the answer. Flavilla spoke the loudest but Clara spoke the fastest.

The big break in our trip came in Sullivan. There we had to take a ferry to get across the bay to Sorrento. Uncle took Brownie out of the buggy thills and led the horse onto the scow. Then we girls backed the two-seater aboard the scow. Aunt followed. While the scow was pulled across the gut by two men rowing a dory, Uncle stood at Brownie's head and spoke reassuring words to him. Reassurance was not needed—the horse held his head high, his ears pricked up. He looked around with all the assurance of a seasoned traveler.

When we were once again on the road and undertaking the last leg of our journey, Uncle gave high praise to Brownie. "A fine horse, right in his prime, always can be trusted, not even thunder frightens him. The only thing that scares him is a horsefly. But we need not worry. I never heard of a horsefly being around in May. They are an August pest."

We ate our lunch before we reached Sorrento. Uncle gave Brownie a box of oats and allowed him to crop the roadside grass and drink from a meadow brook. When at last we drove up the long lane that led to the Brown farmhouse, we saw a strange sight: a man wearing a peanut hat covered with netting was running around with a huge net on the end of a long stick as though to catch butterflies.

Clara was the first to speak. "What is this all about?"

Brownie was the first to know. Several infuriated bees landed on his fat brown rump and stung him. Before Uncle had the time to tighten the reins, Brownie kicked the dashboard out of the buggy with blows that jolted the five of us out of the carriage. Uncle and Flavilla were on the right-hand side of the buggy, and they landed in the soft dirt of the road, but Aunt, Clara, and I were thrown into the bushes. Aunt's hoop was broken and her veil torn. Clara and I were bruised and cut by rose briars. We both bawled. Clara bawled the loudest, and I, the longest. In the meantime, Brownie's good sense returned and he came to a panting halt at the back door.

Aunt Eunice had heard the commotion and she came to the door. When she saw the condition of the buggy and her bedraggled relatives, she burst into loud weeping.

Aunt Eunice looked like Aunt Abigail but it was evident that years of living with her bungling husband had broken her spirit. Aunt Abigail was made of sterner stuff. Leaving Clara and me to the ministrations of Flavilla, she rushed to her sister and pushed her back into the house.

Uncle Otis hurriedly unhitched Brownie, led him into the barn, unharnessed him, and fastened him in a box stall, taking care to check that there were no bees in the stall. Then he went outside to interrogate Uncle Bradford Brown.

It seems that Uncle Bradford had decided to take advantage of the beautiful May morning by dividing a hive of bees. Division had not pleased the colony. Instead of taking up residence in the two hives set for them under the russet tree, the bees had seemingly gone mad. The air between the barn and the house was filled with the angry creatures. As the men talked, one stung Uncle on the ear and another landed on my wrist and I started to bawl all over again.

Bradford Brown's comment was, "It's a shame that this had to happen today. I must have lost the queen bee."

Uncle Otis at once took charge. "Uncle Bradford," he said, "hang that net up in the russet. I believe that you are stirring up the bees and making them madder than ever. Let's go into the house and give them a chance to calm down. Must be an hour before the funeral. We'll work out something."

Uncle Otis and Aunt Abigail devised a plan of operation. Aunt Eunice was too spent from weeping to help. Uncle Bradford's plan had only made a bad matter worse. It was decided that Otis and Flavilla would stand at the end of the lane to warn of the bees in the door yard. Each driver was advised to lead his horse into the yard. The ladies were asked to alight from the carriages and to walk to the front door of the house. Clara and I handed out aprons and towels to be used as head coverings against the attack of the bees.

When it came time for the funeral, Flavilla and Clara joined the mourners in the parlor but I followed Grandma's directions and stayed in the dooryard. I did not mind missing the viewing of the corpse because things in the yard were really exciting. Most of the men chose to stay there, each one standing by the head of his horse. Now and then a bee would sting a horse or his owner. I never saw so many kicking horses. I also heard a lot of words I had never heard before.

Uncle Otis chose to absent himself from the ceremony. He stayed in the yard and went from man to man, offering apologies. I noticed that he was careful to make it clear that he was a relative of Mrs. Brown not Mr. Brown. I also noticed that he made no contradiction when one called Uncle Bradford "a blunderbuss."

When the funeral was over, the hearse and the friends departed, and the family returned from the cemetery, Aunt Abigail made an announcement. "I feel I'm needed here to chirk up Eunice. Clara, tell your father to get Mrs. York to come up to keep house for a few days. Have someone come for me by Sunday. By that time the bees should be over their rampage."

When Clara realized that her mother was not coming home, she started to cry. Her mother spanked her smartly and said, "Stop that howling this minute. I do not intend to raise you to be a Eunice."

We were late in leaving for home. The funeral had not started on time, and our departure had been delayed by Aunt Eunice's tears and Aunt Abigail's directions. At last we drove down the lane. Brownie was pleased to be headed home. Without Uncle's urging, he trotted as though he were eager to get as many miles as possible between himself and the Brown bees.

It was nearly dark when we drove into the Long dooryard. Uncle Joel rushed out to inquire about our lateness. When he saw that the dashboard was missing and that Aunt Abigail was not in the two-seater, his queries changed to laments. And when Uncle Otis and Clara in concert recounted the story of the bees, his laments gave way to profanity. Clara was prompted to remark, "Papa, you would not be talking this way if Mama were here."

Finally Uncle Joel loaned us a lantern and let us go on our way with the eager Brownie drawing the familiar old carriage.

When we got to the Friend place, Grandpa was abed and asleep. Grandma came to the door with a candle in her hand. "I've been so worried," she said. "Where have you been?"

Uncle's answer mystified her. "We've been to funeral bee."

Gran'sir's Boys

When Flavilla came for her fall visit in October of 1852, she did not come alone. David Harding, her cousin, came with her. Like Flavilla, he was the grandchild of one of Grandma's brothers. But unlike Flavilla, he was not having a happy childhood. His father had died; his mother and his older sisters had gone to work in the Augusta cotton mills; David was passed around from family to family where he was neither guest nor family member. Unlike Flavilla, he was not attractive; he was short, his head was very large, and due to a birth injury he walked with a limp. He was bashful and hesitant. When he came into the Friend kitchen, he was uncertain of a welcome. Grandma's kiss helped to reassure him. Grandpa said, "Lad, you are just the boy that I need to help me in my shop." Uncle Otis clapped him on the back and exclaimed, "Welcome, roommate. I've set up a bed for you in my bedroom."

A small bandbox held the few clothes that David owned. He had a Bible, a pocket knife, and a harmonica. But he had other belongings that he valued highly. He had brought with him a crippled cat that he had rescued from a trap. The cat, secured in a crocus bag with her head out, had laid in David's lap all the way from Brooksville. "This is Suzy-blue, my cat," he said as he freed the creature from the bag. "She has only three legs but when the stub of her bad leg heals, she'll earn her board by catching rats and mice."

Grandpa and Grandma were not eager for another cat. We already had several barn cats and Grandma's Tiger ruled the house. But for David's sake, they welcomed Suzy-blue to the house, where she became Tiger's companion.

In a box David had a gander with a broken wing. The great white gander allowed David to lift him out of the box, but he hissed at the strangers who were looking on.

Grandma was delighted with the bird. "David," she said, "a fox caught my gander just last week. My flock of geese will make your gander welcome. The geese are shut up in their yard. Let me show you." The meeting of the geese and the gander was glad and noisy.

By bedtime, David, his cat, and his gander felt quite at home at the Corner.

David's introduction to the schoolchildren of District Seven was not as pleasant as that to my family. At the morning exercises, he did not know the hymn; he stumbled over the words of the Psalm. The teacher found that he read so poorly that she placed him in a reading group of children younger than he. But the worst came at recess time—he was the last child to leave the schoolroom because the teacher had stopped him and questioned him. When he came out of the door, Rob Means and Harrison Whitney were waiting for him. They shouted, "Hello, there, Hop-leg-Harding." Then they laughed loudly and began to limp.

Poor David did not know what to say or to do. But his Cousin Flavilla did. Like an avenging angel, she flew at Robert and Harrison. She cried, "You shall not treat David like this!"

The boys were startled and they used bad strategy. They ran up the road toward the Leith Place with Flavilla in hot pursuit. Robert ran faster than Harrison but the girl overtook both. She first caught up with Harrison and gave him a swift push that toppled him into the ditch. Robert's fate was worse. He was at the edge of Gene's Pond when Flavilla reached him. She caught him off-balance and pushed him into the pond. Flavilla ran back to the schoolyard but the boys made a slow return. Harrison's knees were scraped; Robert was dripping wet. Sam Closson shouted, "Served you right, Rob and Harry." The other children laughed at the bedraggled boys.

There was no more making fun of David. A few days later he was given a name that pleased him and won the approval of Flavilla. In the grove back of the schoolhouse were several tall pine trees. In the top of one was a crow's nest. The young crows had of course taken flight but they often came back to roost in the tree where they had been raised. One day Flavilla said, "David, why don't you show the boys and the girls how you can call crows?"

David had the habit of obedience. While the others stayed in the schoolyard, he went to the grove, where he imitated the call of the crows. In moments, a young crow flew to his feet. The children were surprised and pleased. From that day on they called David "Caw Harding." Joel helped him with his reading so that he was soon able to read with children of his own age. Flavilla and I taught him the words of the Psalms and the hymns. Sam Closson became his special friend and learned how to call crows, though he was not able to imitate the call of the gulls and the owls and the fish hawks as did David.

David was not able to help Grandfather in the shop because he had no knack with tools. Instead, he took over the care of the hens and the geese. Grandma said that the hens had never laid so well as they did under David's care. He took great interest in ailing animals and birds. When one of the cows had a broken horn, he bound it up. When Brownie had a stick in his leg, David removed it and covered the wound with a salt pork poultice. Nor did he limit his interest to the animals of the Friend barnyard. When one of the Grindle oxen was sick, he set up several nights with it and helped to dose it back to health.

Two of the homestead chores Grandma kept for herself. She chose to milk the cows, save for the heifer that Flavilla had frighted. She plucked the live goose feathers. Up overhead in the grain room were barrels of hens' feathers that she used for feather beds and pillows and cushions, but the live goose feathers were kept in a box under her bed. She never had many on hand because whenever she heard that a new baby had been born or that a person was sick, she made a pillow for a gift. "Nothing," she used to declare, "Nothing is as soft as live goose feathers."

Geese, like hens and ducks, shed their feathers in the spring. Grandma kept a sharp eye on the goose yard. When feathers began to blow there, she would say to David, "On Saturday, I shall need you. I plan to pluck the geese."

David did the unskilled work, so to speak. He brought the geese one by one to Grandmother who sat on a milking stool by the barn door. He handed her the goose with the head toward her. Quick as a wink, she put the goose's head under her arm, clamped her left hand around the goose's neck and with her right hand pulled free the loose feathers. She had the goose at her mercy; the bird soon bereft of old feathers and vocal with complaints, was returned to her mates. One by one, David brought the geese; they were plucked until Grandma had several bags of the soft feathers.

The gander from Brooksville recovered from his wing injury and grew into a bird noble in looks and vicious in temper. One year David made a clamp to cover his bill and Grandma made an attempt to pluck him. But the clamp flew off, the bird grabbed Grandma's arm, and he was returned to the goose yard with all his feathers. Uncle liked to tease Grandmother about her failure and he made up a song.

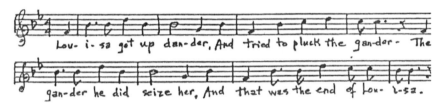

Lou-i-sa got up dan-der, And tried to pluck the gan-der. The gan-der he did seize her, And that was the end of Lou-i-sa.

When Flavilla returned home in November, David did not go with her. I never heard my grandparents discuss David's status or future. It was Uncle Joel Long who finally brought up the issue. Looking back, I can see that Uncle Joel often precipitated issues. One January evening he dropped in for a call. Aunt Abigail had not come with him. Had she been there, he would not have said what he did. We were sitting in front of the kitchen fire; Grandma was knitting, Uncle and Grandpa were whittling spiles for tapping maples, David and I were writing on our slates. In a lull in the talk, Uncle Joel said, "It must cost a lot to feed and clothe David. You are kind, John, to take in a stranger."

David turned very red; Grandpa and Uncle Otis stopped their work; Grandma knitted faster than ever. "Joel," she said, "David more than earns his board and bed. He is no stranger. He is one of the family. This is his home."

The following spring, the little bedroom off Uncle's room was cleared of boxes and trunks and became David's room where he kept his collection of feathers and eggs and shells. Grandmother gave him geese and hens' eggs to set so that he had eggs of his own to sell. By summer my grandparents were calling him "son." He grew taller and his head no longer seemed too large for him. He was no longer hesitant and bashful. Of course he always limped, but he no longer needed Flavilla to fight his battles.

David Harding was not the only boy who found shelter at Grandfather Friend's.

Philip Melancen was a boy from New York who had shipped as cabin boy on Captain John Miller's schooner. When Captain Miller tied up for the winter, Philip was marooned at McHeard's with no money to get him home. Captain Miller offered him board and bed but Philip was not happy with the Millers. The boy was homesick and miserable. He hung around Uncle Joel's gristmill and it was there that he met Grandpa and David. One day he asked if he could winter at the Corner. Captain Miller was willing; Grandfather agreed; so Philip came to our house and became David's companion and bedfellow.

Philip was less miserable at our house but he was still homesick. There was nothing that interested him. He was smart in school but did not like to read and figure. He did his chores quickly but he took no joy in doing them. He could play ball or checkers or jack-draws but he preferred to watch others play.

Philip's favorite expression was, "making arrangements." One day he went to the shore and was gone a long time. When he came back to the house he remarked, "I've been making arrangements to dig clams." He talked of "making arrangements" to dig gum, to set traps, to catch trout and to weave baskets. To my knowledge, he never did any of them.

Finally, Grandmother interested the homesick boy in baking. When she baked cookies in the tin baker in front of the blazing fire, she asked Philip to watch the cookies. It was a task that he liked. In time, Grandma promoted him to mixing and rolling and cutting the cookies.

In February of 1854 Mother and Par Giles came home for a few weeks between voyages. My father felt that Philip was Captain Miller's responsibility and he voiced his views to the captain. My mother felt that Philip was more work that he was help but she was sorry for the homesick boy and she wrote to his Sunday School teacher telling her of Philip's unhappiness. It was months before an answer came. In fact, the answer came three months later when my parents were again at home between-trips. The teacher enclosed in her letter money to pay for Philip's return to New York.

After the letter came, Philip appeared like a different lad. He talked about "making arrangements" to go home. He did make preparations: he packed his belongings in the bandbox that David gave him; he asked Uncle Otis to cut his hair; he made farewell calls on the Corner neighbors. Grandma and Mother cut up an old jacket of my father's and made Philip a new coat for the trip home. Grandma gave him a pair of woolen stockings and Grandpa gave him a wallet with coins in it. Father took him to the wharf to meet the steamboat to Rockland.

When my father came back from the wharf, he remarked, "I got Captain Miller's one-time cabin boy safely headed for home. We shall never again see Philip Melancen."

Father was wrong. Some twenty years later he took his schooner, laden with long lumber, into New York harbor. One day, as he watched men unload the lumber, a tall young man came up to him and asked, "Are you Captain Giles Wood from Blue Hill?"

Father admitted his identity but he did not recognize his questioner. The young man was Philip Melancen, a prosperous baker, one of whose shops was on the waterfront.

The man asked my father about the Friends and the neighbors at the Corner. He sent his greetings and he took special care to inquire Father's sailing date. "I shall have a box," he said, "that I shall ask you to take to the Friends for me. I often think of their kindnesses to me. I realize that I did not earn my salt when I stayed with them."

The big box that Philip sent us held pound cakes and fruit cakes and plum cakes, all wrapped in layers of cloth; molasses bars filled with raisins and dates; bags of nuts; jars of tea and candied fruits. Grandma shared the treats with the Clossons and the Grindles. It pleased her to remark, "I take the credit for providing New York City with a baker."

In the 1840s and 1850s, towns bid off the poor to the lowest bidder. To please David, Grandpa bid in a pauper boy named Nelson Staples from Brooksville. He had once been David's playmate. Nelson was not contented at the Corner. After a time, he ran away and went to sea.

John Brackett was another boy whom Grandfather bid in. I think he was from Sedgwick. He stayed several years and was a fine, capable worker. It was he who called Grandfather "Gran'sir." The name pleased others, and soon my grandfather was known as Gran'sir Friend. It was my father who called the boys who came to live with us "Gran'sir's boys."

I can not recall the names of all of the boys. In warm weather they slept in the shed chamber—in cold weather, in Uncle Otis's room. When the school was in session, they attended it. They went to the church with the family. They shared the meals and the evening sociability before the fire. On election day and on Christmas day they were given coins. Grandma knit and sewed for them. They had free time for fishing and hunting and skating. When they left to earn their own living, Grandmother supplied them with new stockings and mittens; Grandfather gave them tools and a few gold pieces.

Grandfather's boys had a good home at the Corner, but there is no doubt that they earned their bed and board. Every summer they helped Grandfather with the porgy chores. It was work that Uncle Otis was glad to give up to the boys. He always said, "There is nothing in the world that smells as bad as boiling porgies."

Grandfather's lower field edged the bay and was called the saltwater meadow. It sloped steeply to the cove and to Porgy Point to the west. Grandfather's fish shack, a gray shingled building smelling of tar and fish, was by the shore. It was large enough so that in winter it sheltered the peapod, pulled up in November lest it be caught in the winter ice. On the walls of the shack were shelves that held boxes of twine, hooks, reels, and sinkers. The corners were piled with oars and nets.

Grandma never liked to have me go to the shack to play. "You come home all smelled up. Even your hair smells of fish," she used to say.

She did, however, allow me to play in the field while Grandfather and his boys tended the weir or worked on the shore and in the fish house. On a big rock in the meadow I had a colony of shells—father shells, mother shells, and children shells. I made burdock furniture for them and gathered mullein leaves to serve as "woolen blankets" for their beds. I always returned to the house with welk stains on my hands and burdocks on my skirt.

Long before I was born, Grandfather had built a weir from the end of the point to the eastern side of the cove. Uncle Otis liked to recall the April bee when the pilings were driven into the flats. Five or six men did the job using a handmade pile-driver. Sticks were driven between the piles and joined together with birch or spruce "ribbons"—actually rails. Then brush was woven into the "ribbons" to make the weir "fish tight."

Every spring the weir had to be repaired. I planned to be on deck to watch the work. Tar was heated in a big iron kettle, then pieces of netting were dipped into the hot tar. At low tide the boys rowed out to the weir with brush and netting to repair the holes that had developed during the winter. Over the years, the marine growth that encrusted the bushes and ribbons tightened the weir.

Porgy runs came in July and August. Oddly enough, there were none after 1879. Likely the food supply of the porgies played out. Porgies are a fatty fish, something like mackerel. We used them for bait; we never ate them—no more than we did horse mackerel. Grandpa caught the fish for their oil. When he had a good catch in the weir, the boys rowed out and brought the fish to the shore where they were boiled in iron kettles. Most likely the kettles held twenty gallons. It was some sight to watch the roaring fire of burning driftwood and alders, to see the clouds of steam rising from the boiling fish and to hear the gulls screaming overhead, drawn from miles around by the stench of the boiling fish. Once the fish were cooked, they were shoveled into a press. The round, blocklike cover of the press was turned, and out poured the yellow oil that was caught in pails and then poured into barrels.

The filled barrels were later taken on the jigger to Uncle Joel's wharf. In September, a porgy schooner came from Rockland and picked up the barrels for delivery in Boston, where the oil was used to make paint. The Rockland captain paid cash to Grandfather and the other farmers who produced the oil. Grandfather always said, "Porgy oil is a cash-on-the-barrel-head crop."

A small cask of the oil was taken to the barn cellar and stored there. It was great for oiling guns and machinery. It was a good cleaner, too. It would take any stain off hands—even tar.

Grandfather used the flesh of the boiled porgies as fertilizer. He and the boys spread it on the fields, but the gulls gulped down a lot of it. David tried to teach Painter to chase off the gulls. The dog knew what was expected of him, but he felt that gull chasing was beneath his dignity. Besides, he did not like to step on the porgy mash.

While Grandpa and his helpers were working with the porgies, they had to do a lot of dressing and undressing. Grandma supplied them with old clothing to wear at the shore. Before they came into the house, they were expected to go to the barn, bathe, and change their clothes. When the porgy season was over, David washed and boiled the porgy drawers, shirts and pantaloons and spread them in the meadow to dry. "I won't have porgy pants dried on my clothes line," declared Grandmother.

Grandmother depended upon Gran'sir's boys to supply her with fish for the table. At the Cunner Rock they caught cunners for chowder. They caught flounders on Mr. Grindle's dock. Fried flounders make a good breakfast.

In late April and early May smelts swam up the brooks and left their eggs. Sometimes I was allowed to go with Uncle Otis and the boys when they went smelting. We went after dark on the full of the tide and we took a burning pitch knot to light our way. The boys carried nets nailed to barrel hoops. We usually went to the neighborhood brook that drained the Leith Spring, I held the torch while Uncle and the boys dipped out the small fish that shone like silver.

Tinker mackerel came into the bay in July and August and they bit best on a cloudy day. We toled them to the boat by throwing out "chum"—chopped up clams. Tinkers are blue in color and are very lively. It was fun to catch them. Now and then Uncle and David borrowed Uncle Joel's sailboat and went beyond the islands to catch haddock, cod, and hake.

Some of the fish were cured or pickled for winter use. The surplus smelts were dried on the canvas-covered roof of the sheep pen. Cod, haddock and hake were sun dried on flakes and lightly salted. The fish thus cured were called "stripped fish." Some folks stored the stripped fish in the haymow. Grandma hung hers in the cheese room. They were never kept in the cellar for they would be sure to mold there. The largest of the mackerel were cleaned and strung on lathes that were hung in the smokehouse for a slow smoking. Grandma "put down" some of the mackerel in crocks filled with a liquor of vinegar and spices. We were fond of pickled fish because the vinegar caused the bones to soften.

It was always easy for Uncle or one of the boys to grab a "rocker" and a clam hook and go to the shore for a mess of clams. Uncle "shocked" the clams, Grandma chopped the raw clams and made the chowder, then we all ate it with much smacking of lips. Now and then a hard winter froze up the bay; a stiff blow came and piled up huge ice cakes on the beach. When that happened, the family had to go without clam chowder. Then Grandpa lamented, "What I wouldn't give for a mess of clams!"

The Friends never made any account of lobsters. Just for fun Grandfather's boys now and then clawed out a few from under the rocks. David boiled them, pounded them up and fed them to his hens, who seemed to regard the fish as a treat. Later, David found that folks in the village liked lobsters and would buy them from him. He worked up quite a little trade selling lobsters, small ones, two for five cents, the large ones, five cents.

Nor did the family eat trout. The boys caught trout because they enjoyed a tramp along Peters' Brook. Grandma boiled their catch and fed it to the cats.

Gran'sir's boys were taught the care of sheep. There were always a dozen or so of the animals on the farm, enough to provide wool for Grandma to spin into yarn that she knit into mittens and stockings. Once she knit two suits of underwear for Grandpa—shirts and drawers that lasted for decades. The sheep pen was half way up the steep field to the east of the house. Around it was a yard divided from the field by a cedar fence. Even in the coldest days of winter, the sheep had the freedom of the yard, where they bunched together in the sunshine or dug for "old fog" under the snow.

The sheep lambed in April, always an exciting time for me because usually there was an ailing lamb brought into the kitchen for nursing and "cosseting." One year there were twin rams that caused a lot of talk and got a lot of attention. I remember that they were born the spring of 1857, not long after a new president and vice-president had taken office. Uncle Otis named the lambs Buchanan and Breckenridge for our executives.

In early May, the sheep were sheared. First the lambs were caught and put outside the yard, where they circled unhappily, bleating for their mothers. Grandfather, Uncle Otis, and David worked together shearing the sheep. A sheep was caught, two legs on one side were tied together to discourage kicking, and then she was pushed back on her haunches. Grandfather sheared the creature while Uncle and David held her down. They talked reassuringly to the sheep and often sang. Grandfather started cutting at the sheep's neck and then worked down the animal's body, always holding the blade of the shears away from the sheep lest he cut the flesh. Try as best he could, there were always a few cuts. Grandma stood ready with a pail of hen's grease and a rag with which to daub grease on the cut. After a sheep was sheared, she looked naked and forlorn, standing in the center of a rug of curly wool.

After all the sheep were sheared, the lambs were taken back to the yard. For a few minutes the young ones appeared not to recognize their mothers. There was always a lot of running and bawling and nudging before each lamb was reunited with its mother.

In late May the sheep and the lambs were taken to Darling Island to spend the summer and fall. This chore took all day and required some extra help. Either the Closson boys or Uncle Joel's sons came to help.

Soon after breakfast, the sheep were caught and their legs tied together. Grandfather took pains to tie up a sheep and her lamb at the same time. When eight or nine creatures were tied up, they were lifted into the jigger and driven "under the hill," by the Means place, to the cove opposite Darling Island. Three of the sheep were transferred to a rowboat, where they lay helpless on the bottom of the boat. While Uncle and one of the boys rowed the boat to the island, Grandfather and another boy went back to the Corner for more sheep. A boy and I stayed on the shore with the sheep waiting for the next trip to the island.

Darling Island was perhaps three hundred yards from the shore and so I had a clear view of the unloading of the sheep. I had to laugh at the way they acted when they were untied. Up a sheep jumped, leaped into the air, and landed on stiff legs. In no time at all, they were all grazing. The old sheep remembered the island from the preceding summer and soon led their lambs to the spring.

This all had to be done in reverse in the fall. By October the sheep were pretty wild because they had been alone all summer. Uncle always had a crew of four or five boys to chase the sheep down. Grandfather took pains to caution him, "Now try not to frighten the sheep or to be rough with them when you tie them up. Don't overtire them. Whatever you do, don't drive one off a rock. You know how easy it is for a sheep to break a leg."

Uncle's reply was always the same: "I'll do my best, Father. But I wish that you would caution the sheep not to overtire ME or break MY leg."

One year a sheep got loose in the boat and fell overboard. Had not David jumped into the water to rescue her, she would have drowned, pulled down by the weight of her wet wool.

The men were always relieved when the sheep were safely back in the home pen. After one October sheep transfer that had been especially tiring and vexing, I said to my uncle, "I expect if the music master had been here today, he would have sung songs."

I have always remembered Uncle's reply, "Hannah, a man who has chased sheep all day does not have breath enough left to cool his soup, much less to sing a song."

Grandpa Friend was more than farmer and fisherman. In a small way, he was a quarryman. Mr. Grindle had showed him how to handle powder, drill stone, and break granite into rectangular paving. Grandfather never allowed the boys to handle the powder, but he taught them to use drills and hammers. Every year they broke up a few meadow and pasture boulders and cut them into paving to sell to Mr. Grindle. He had a contract to supply paving for the New Orleans streets. He bought paving from his neighbors; he quarried granite in his pasture and had men square up the pieces. Some of the grout—waste granite—he had used to make a small dock from which he shipped the paving. There were pieces of waste stone all around the neighborhood. Folks used them for walls and for the foundation of outhouses.

My grandfather took pains to teach his boys how to use tools, though only John Brackett was really handy with them. All of them learned how to chop and cut wood with axes, adzes and broadaxes. They knew the use of augers and mallets and beetles. They handled Grandfather's square and plumb level. But his shoemaking tools were not touched by the boys. Though Grandfather now and then made shoes for Grandmother or me, he used to say sadly, "The day of the home cobbler is over. Those shoe shops in western Maine have put us out of business."

All of Gran'sir's boys were interested in politics and elections because they listened to the grown-ups reading aloud from the papers: the weeklies—the *Belfast Republican* and the Ellsworth paper—and the semi-weekly from Bangor. When Mother and Par Giles came home, they brought papers from Portland or Boston or New York and sometimes from Charleston and the Islands. Articles, often long outdated, were read aloud and thoroughly discussed. The boys heard their elders talk politics. The Clossons, the Grindles, and the Friends were Whigs. Uncle Zenas took no part in the political talk. When questioned about his views, he replied, "I think just as Mr. Grindle does."

Mr. Grindle's brand of Whiggery was not identical with that of my grandparents. Likely because he sold paving to the South, he was temperate in his attitude toward slavery. Grandmother Friend belonged to the American Antislavery Society. She condemned slavery and indicted the slaveowners as "evil, wicked men." Grandfather would not argue with his neighbor, Mr. Grindle, but Grandma would. She welcomed "a spat with Mil," as she called her vocal exchanges with her neighbor. Grandfather and Uncle Otis would not listen to them. Uncle went to his room and fiddled; Grandpa excused himself by saying that he had to go to the barn to look after the stock. David and I stayed in the kitchen to look and to listen. Grandma's ears got very red; Mr. Grindle shouted and pounded the table. I always felt that Grandma won because she quoted so many Abolitionists: Garrison, The Grimke Sisters and even Enoch Pond, who lived right in nearby Bucksport.

Uncle Joel Long was a Democrat and a staunch one. Indeed, he was a staunch supporter of every cause in which he believed. He and Aunt Abigail often called at Grandfather's. Usually Grandpa and Aunt Abigail could steer Grandma and Uncle away from a political collision. But if Mr. Grindle chanced to drop in, a political storm brewed and broke. The three partisans argued over the tariff, the codfish bounty, and the extension of slavery. The battle was suspended only when Aunt Abigail said, "Joel, if you do not hitch up and take me home, I shall walk."

The young folks followed the lead of their elders. Gran'sir's boys, the Closson children, and I were loyal Whigs. The Long children—Moses, George and Clara—were Democrats. When the Corner children went to McHeard's, the Long children shouted at us, "Whigs, Whigs, you eat pigs."

We shouted right back at them, "Democrats, Democrats, eat dead rats."

Uncle Otis and John Brackett liked to do carpenter work and often had the chance to work out by the day. Now and then they worked for Uncle Joel on a schooner. For two summers they worked for Mr. Grindle to help him build a barn.

Mr. Grindle did much of the work himself. He dug the barn cellar out of a side hill so that two sides of the cellar wall were dirt; the other two sides were built of granite blocks quarried in the Grindle pasture. He set two girder posts in the center of the dirt floor. Across them he stretched the girder on which rested the joists that supported the floor. The floor boards were left unnailed. The ends of the girders and joists fitted into mortises cut in the sills that topped the dirt and rock walls.

Mr. Grindle cut his own timber for the barn. He cut oak and pine trees and squared them with a broadaxe. These became sills, beams, joists and "bents." Boards for the floor were cut at Uncle Joel's mill.

It was Uncle Otis who put together the five braced sections, called "bents," that were later raised to make the framework of the barn. He put the bents together with pegs driven into place by a forty-pound beetle.

I liked to go with Uncle when he worked at Grindle's. There was a new baby there and I was allowed to hold her. "Aunt Belinda" always treated us with cookies and milk. I took care to avoid Gyp, the family horse, who was known to nip visitors whom he regarded as trespassers. Against the workshop grew pink and white hollyhocks. I liked to gather the little round seedpods, which I called "cheeses." I kept them in my skirt pocket and now and then ate one.

But best of all, I liked to sit near Uncle Otis and watch him work. He often paused to talk with me. He pointed at the peglike endings on the base of the pinned framework and explained that they would be set in holes on the sills. He explained, "A pulley with ropes will pull up the bents and men with long pikes will them in place."

My eyes grew big with wonder when my uncle told that the pikes held by the men would be sixteen feet long, that women and children would come for the barn raising, that there would be a picnic in the field. I felt that I just could not wait for the day of the barn raising.

On the day of the barn raising both the school at McHeard's and at the Corner were closed so that the masters could help with pikes and hammers and the children could enjoy the fun and the excitement. Mr. Grindle tied up Gyp in our barn. The oxen were tethered in the field and they watched the work with great dignity. Using sawhorses and planks, the men built tables to hold the food. A cask of sweet cider stood by the door of the barn cellar. Beside it was a bushel basket filled with Aunt Belinda's molasses doughnuts.

The men brought their own tools and set to work with a will on raising the bents. The women unpacked baskets of food, bustled about the kitchen and refilled the doughnut basket. We children were ordered to stay away from the barn lest we get in the way or be hit by a falling timber. We played tag and hide-and-go-seek and snap-the-whip. At noontime we were each given a plate and a spoon; we helped ourselves helter-skelter to beef stew and beans and corn bread and biscuits. We later came back for squares of cake and wedges of pie.

After dinner, the boys retreated to the woods to gather nuts. We girls sat in the field and watched the men at work. Sarah Miller brought us boughs of maples. We picked off the red and yellow leaves and fastened them together using the stems as pins. We decked the four oxen with our streamers and the patient creatures seemed to enjoy our attention. When Uncle Otis saw what we were doing, he called to us,

"Girls, make a long leaf rope. Before we raise the last bent, I'll nail the rope to the top and it will be a banner of celebration."

It was late afternoon before the last bent was swung up and lifted into place. On its top fluttered our festoon of leaves. The women and the children in the field were silent as they watched. As the framework of the barn stood complete, Uncle Otis shouted the old lines,

> Here is a good frame.
> It deserves a good name.
> What shall we call it?

Men and women and children shouted back, "Milford Grindle's barn!"

At Home and Away

Father liked to have company. He also liked to be company. He had no near relatives living in town. His brothers were in California and his sisters in Dover, New Hampshire, where they worked in a coat shop. But he did have numerous first and second cousins in the village. He called on each of them, taking gifts, sugar or raisins or a bag of coffee beans. I once heard Grandma say, "Giles gives things away just about as fast as he can bring them home."

Calling around did not satisfy the Captain's desire for sociability, so he suggested that he take Grandfather and Grandmother to Sedgwick to visit Grandfather's younger brothers, William and Robert. He made the suggestion at the supper table. I could tell by the gleam in Grandpa's eyes that he liked the idea. But before he could reply Grandma said, "Oh, no. I cannot go. Who would milk the cows and tend the milk?"

When Mother allowed that she could milk the cows and do the dairy chores, Grandma said, "But I've never been away from Hannah."

This time my father answered, "But Hannah will have her mother to look after her. Much as Hannah loves you, she won't need you."

By this time Grandfather was able to speak and he had the last word: "Louisa, I would really like to see my brothers. I shall have a better time if you are with me. Please go."

Grandma consented to go on the visit but she insisted that she could not leave until she had churned and done up the butter. Tuesday she had Mother watch her milking and she gave her directions: "Remember that you have to watch Buttercup or she will switch her tail in the pail. Be sure to talk to Clover. Listening makes her let down her milk better. And don't forget to pour milk into Joe's and Jed's saucers."

Grandma's instructions were not confined to the barn chores. She reminded us to feed Tiger, to close the windows if a shower came up, and to keep the water pails filled. She charged Otis, "Don't use cream on your oatmeal." She advised Mother, "See to it that you are all in bed by eight o'clock."

On Wednesday morning when the folks left for Sedgwick, Grandma's last bidding was, "Eliza, be sure to wind the clock."

I felt sad when I watched Grandpa, Grandma, and Par Giles drive out of the yard. When Mother noticed that my chin was trembling, she grabbed my hand and said, "Run and we'll beat your uncle back to the kitchen."

My sadness gave way to amazement when I saw the way my mother laid out the work. "We won't make the beds, Hannah. Turn the clothes back over the footboard. We'll let the sun and the fresh air sweeten the sheets."

"But Grandma..," I began.

"Never mind Grandma," interrupted my mother, "When she comes back on Friday afternoon, the beds will be made and there will be no dust in the corners. Until then we'll do only what we have to do in the house. I plan to help Otis hoe the potato patch in the back field. You can go with us and play in the woods."

"And leave the house?" I asked.

"Of course we'll leave the house. No one will take it away," replied Mother.

The house in fact got little attention for the next two days. We even ate in the back yard. "Eating alfresco," Mother called it. She said that the rich people in the South did it that way. She had Uncle haul some of the banking boards round to the back door for a floor. She and I moved out the kitchen table and three chairs. We had our breakfasts there with a large pitcher of cream in the center of the table. Uncle just drowned his cereal in cream. She cooked no vegetables. She baked dropped biscuits and cooked meat and eggs. We ate the sweets that Par Giles had cooked for us. We washed dishes only once a day.

On Wednesday and Thursday evening she asked the Closson children to come in. There was no treat for them but they did not mind. She taught them to dance, using the banking boards as the dance floor. Otis played a tune on his violin. He hummed and sang,

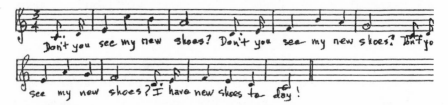

Don't you see my new shoes? Don't you see my new shoes? Don't you see my new shoes? I have new shoes to day!

Mother first danced with Joel. He was full of music and caught on to the steps. Then Joel taught Kate while Mother danced with Sam. Before the evening was over there were three couples dancing on the banking boards. When I became too tired to dance, Otis took my place and we made our own music by singing real loud. It was way after nine o'clock before the children started for home. They met Uncle Zenas at the brook but he did not scold them for being late.

Friday morning Mother was all business. She was up extra early and by mid-morning had made the beds, swept, and scrubbed up the kitchen floor. She put all the milk pans against the shed's outer wall to sun. Otis put away the banking boards. He busied himself currying Brownie, cleaning out the barn, and hoeing the peas and the corn. After dinner Mother made cookies, the sour cream kind, and layer cake that she topped with whipped cream. She soaked out dried fish and boiled potatoes so that we could have hash for supper. When she finished her work, she said, "I'm sure, Hannah, that your grandmother will be pleased with everything. True the cream jug is at low ebb but I know what we'll do. After we've changed our dresses, we'll walk over to Uncle Zenas's, I have coins, and I know that Mrs. Closson will be glad to sell us a quart of sweet cream. If she sells sweet cream there will be less sour cream to churn. She really does not like to make butter."

I watched for the folks from the front yard. When I saw them coming, I ran to meet them. Par Giles hauled up Whitey and I climbed aboard. Grandma asked so many questions that I could not answer them. After she went into the house she walked from room to room looking at everything. "Seems as though the oleander has grown while I've been away," she said.

I followed my grandmother when she went into the buttery. The first thing she did was to take the cover off the cream jug. She nodded, smiled, and complimented my mother, "Eliza, you have done well. The house is all in trim and the cream jug filled to the brim. You and Otis look so rested that I'm sure that you went to bed early."

When I began to say, "But, Grandma, we didn't..," Otis interrupted me to remark, "Louisa, trim and brim rhyme. Do you know that you made a poem?"

"No, I don't know that," she replied, "and there is another thing that I do not know—how your sister managed to make sour cream cookies and whipped cream cake and yet save all the cream that she did."

Mother did not know what to say but Par Giles helped her out. "Louisa," he said, "don't try to understand everything. Just be glad that your cream cup runneth over."

I was included in the next trip that Par Giles got up. Mother got word that her uncle, Al Tibbetts, was in bed with his last sickness. Father felt that both she and Otis should go to see him. Otis spoke to Joel Closson and got him to come over and help Grandfather with the chores and the hoeing.

We made great preparations for our journey to Brooksville. For two days Whitey was given a complete rest so that he would be fresh for the trip. Par Giles borrowed Mr. Grindle's two-seated buggy. I repacked my little satchel two or three times a day. I put in it my best blue calico, the red slippers that Grandpa had made for me, my brush and comb, and the new nightie that Grandma had trimmed with knitted lace. I left room for Tabitha, my doll, and her clothes.

Father filled his largest firkin with supplies from the pantry. This time Grandma was eager to give. She urged, "Be sure to take some vanilla and curry powder; a new flavor might tempt Alvin's appetite. And why don't you take the bottle of wine on the top of the shelf? I approve of using wine as medicine."

Mother made up a small box of gifts for Aunt May. She put in the box a length of blue calico, a square of linen, and some spools of thread. "Poor May," said Mother, "I feel sorry for her. She lost all her babies save one and now she is going to lose her husband."

"I've always felt sorry for her," spoke up Grandma, "She trots, trots all day and yet never gets her work done. She was real good working in a sail loft but she's no housekeeper. I hope that her stepdaughter Lena has come home to help her."

The morning that we left for the Tibbettses Grandma got together her own gifts. She sent three pounds of butter wrapped in large rhubarb leaves, a bunch of sage, a jar of apple butter and a box of mince turnovers. "I remember that Al always liked turnovers but I expect that he is now too low to eat pastries," she said.

We left for Brooksville soon after breakfast. Uncle and Par Giles sat on the front seat; Mother and I on the back with a faded umbrella over our heads. My grandparents watched us drive out of the yard. Grandpa said nothing but Grandma called after us, "Take a good look at the pond for me."

As we neared the Head-of-the-Bay, Par Giles suggested stopping to see Aunt Rebecca. "We go right by her house at the top of the hill. Seems as though we ought to pause."

Mother was agreeable but Uncle objected: "If we stop, it will mean we'll be on the road at high noon when it will be real hot. We didn't bring a lunch and so ought to be at Uncle's by dinnertime."

Father and Mother were guided by Uncle's objections and it was decided that we would not stop at the Friend-Darling house.

But as we neared the house we saw two women behind the picket fence. Mrs. Darling was on her knees pulling weeds. Aunt Rebecca was standing in the shade watching her sister. "Oh, bother," said Uncle, "now we'll have to stop."

Par Giles guided Whitey into the yard and all four of us got out of the carriage. Uncle unfastened Whitey's check rein and stood by the horse's head. My parents and I went into the yard, where I took pains to stand beside Mrs. Darling. When she heard that we were on our way to visit a sick relative, she exclaimed, "Oh, I must have something to send to the sick man. Hannah, come into the house with me and we'll see what we can find."

She took a freshly baked loaf of bread from the shelf and wrapped it in a new towel. She went down cellar and came back with a bottle of dandelion wine. Then she picked up a pot of red geraniums from the window sill. "This will be for the poor wife," she said, "she will need a bit of brightness at a time like this."

Our call was a short one. We were soon on our journey.

"Mrs. Darling was very generous," said my mother.

"I notice that Rebecca sent nothing," added Father.

"The only thing that I ever knew her to give away was a bad cold," commented Uncle Otis.

Mother scolded her brother, "Otis you should be ashamed of yourself. I am glad that Louisa did not hear you talk that way."

Our trip to Brooksville took us up hill and down dale. The men walked up the steep hills to make it easier for Whitey. When we came to a spring we stopped to water the horse. Once we drove horse and carriage right out into a wide brook and uncle walked along the thill to unfasten Whitey's check rein. We rested for a bit under the shade of an oak that grew at the edge of the brook. On the top of Kenches's mountain, really a steep hill, we got out of the carriage to pick blueberries. Par Giles made a birch bark basket so that we could pick some "pie fodder" for Aunt May.

Even with all our stops we got to the Tibbetts farmhouse by noontime. It was a Cape Cod house built on a knoll that overlooked Walker's Pond. As we drove up the lane to the house we saw a young woman in the garden picking peas. She wore a big pink sunbonnet. I had never seen one before, and this one seemed very elegant to me. She set down her basket and hurried to the lane to show us the way to the barn. She had a round face with very pink cheeks. When she smiled at us she showed deep dimples in her cheeks. She spoke sadly to us, "You must be Cousin Eliza, Otis, and Captain Wood. I'm your Cousin Lena. I've come home to help my stepmother with father. The doctor says that it won't be long now. Drive right into the barn with the horse. I'll go into the house with Eliza and Hannah."

We went into the kitchen through a long woodshed and summer pantry. Everything was out of order. I decided that our Brooksville relatives had never heard of Grandpa's rule, "A place for everything and everything in its place." In the kitchen, Aunt May greeted us. She was tall with graying hair, big hands, and swollen feet. She wore a gray calico dress and wiped her hands on her worn apron as she talked with us. She talked in a dull tone but she was pleased with the boxes of gifts that my father and uncle brought to her. We were guided into the parlor bedroom to see Uncle Al, who lay in a spool bed with his head and shoulders on a high pile of pillows. He reached out eager hands to welcome us and said, "I've made my last load of hay."

I was glad to get out of the sickroom and go with Lena to finish picking the peas. I couldn't take my eyes off her pink sunbonnet. As she gathered peas she talked to me about her work at the sail loft in Bucksport, about the trout that she liked to catch in the meadow brook, about winter skating on the pond, and about the annual ice cutting in the neighborhood. I listened, but I was thinking about the bonnet and how much I would like to have one.

When we went back into the house, Lena threw the bonnet on the kitchen sofa. I sat on the sofa and fingered the bonnet while my mother and Lena shelled the peas. We ate dinner in the kitchen and I was unable to keep my eyes on the object of my devotion. In the afternoon Lena took me for a walk to the Colby's where there was a little boy named Napoleon who was just my age. I was not used to playing tag with a boy and I was frightened by "Boney's" shouting and pushing. I was relieved when we started to walk back to Uncle Al's. I got up my courage and said to Cousin Lena, "Do little girls wear sunbonnets?"

Her reply was, "Perhaps so. But I did not have one when I was a child."

After supper we all sat in Uncle Al's room but I placed my chair near the door so that I could look out into the kitchen and see Lena's bonnet on its wooden peg. When we went to bed, Aunt May went to the kitchen to finish her work. Par Giles offered to sit up with the sick man so that Aunt May could rest. As Mother helped me slip my nightie over my head, she said, "Things are sad here. After Uncle Al dies, Lena will go back to the shop, Aunt May will go back to her folks, and the place will be sold. My mother's generation will be all gone and there will be no one to love and care for the old homestead where so many of the family have been born and have died."

Things were more cheerful in the morning. Uncle Al was more comfortable. Aunt May had caught up with her housework. It was cooler. When we left for the Corner, there was a present for each of us; Captain Tibbett's compass for father, a music book for Uncle, and a pink luster mug for mother. But my gift was the best—Lena tied on my head a pink sunbonnet that she had made the previous night while I slept. I was too pleased to say thank you and had to be prompted by my mother.

We had a cool trip home and a fast one. Whitey seemed to know that we were headed for the familiar barn. But I would not have complained had the trip been hot and slow. The possession of the bonnet put me above the consideration of heat and speed. When we at last reached the home dooryard, I was the first one out of the carriage. I raced into the house to show my grandmother my new headgear. When I played in the yard, I wore it. When I went to bed, it was on my head. When I went to church, I wore it, too.

Uncle Otis liked to tease me about my bonnet. "It has been so long since I have seen my niece's face that I have forgotten the color of her eyes," he said.

The Music Master

Flavilla was not our only guest in the spring of 1852. The music master also spent two weeks with us. The music school was planned by two men at the village. Jonah Holt and George Stevens were very interested in children even though Mr. Holt had only one child, a frail daughter, and Mr. Stevens had none. They got up a subscription paper to pay for a singing teacher. It was their idea to have the school meet three evenings a week at the schoolhouse at McHeard's, and three evenings a week at the Academy at the Head-of-the-Bay. For four weeks of teaching the master was to be paid twenty dollars and "found."

Mr. Holt and Mr. Stevens were too busy with their stores and lumbering and shipbuilding to go around with a subscription paper, but they sent Mr. Stevens's nephew, John Albert Stevens. The nephew arrived at our house just at dinner time and he was asked to draw up and eat pork scraps and potatoes. While he ate, he talked. John Albert was a poor solicitor. He dulled the urgency of his request by saying, "Of course if the subscribers don't come up with the twenty dollars, Uncle George and Jonah will make up the odds."

Grandpa was hesitant to make a pledge, but prompted by Grandma he finally said, "Between us, my son Otis and I will give one dollar; the master can stay here as long as he likes."

Grandma added her approval, "We'll be glad to have the master. I'd like to have Hannah attend the singing school. Her mother and father would be tremendous proud to have her make progress in singing."

The twenty dollars was raised, partly by subscription and partly by Holt and Stevens donations. A master from Unity was hired with the arrangement that he would hold school Monday, Tuesday, and

Wednesday evenings at the village and Thursday, Friday, and Saturday evenings at McHeard's. All children and young people were invited to attend whether or not their folks had given money. Because Friend's Corner was between the two meeting places, Grandfather's was selected as the master's boarding place.

The Saturday before the master's arrival was a busy day. Grandma readied my parent's room for the master. Otis cleared out a box stall for the master's horse. I was doubtful about Brownie's and Whitey's treatment of a strange animal, but Uncle reassured me, "Maybe the horse will be a mare who will cheer up old bachelors like our horses."

Uncle did not like it very well when I remarked, "Cheer you up too. You are a bachelor."

His crisp reply was, "Not really."

The master came late Sunday afternoon. Grandpa was sitting at the west window reading Psalms and so was the first to see the master and his black mare. "There he is now," Grandfather called, "and his carriage is loaded to the gunwales."

Uncle rushed out to greet the stranger and to suggest that he drive to the front door to unload his dunnage.

The master did not long remain a stranger. After he had driven to the house, he jumped lightly over the wheel, handed the reins to Otis, and came to the door to shake hands with Grandfather and Grandmother. He was tall, blond, and slender. His eyes were gray and he had a deep dimple in one cheek.

As he grasped my grandparents' hands, he introduced himself, "I am John Lamb from Unity. I am free, white, and unmarried, and I sing to put myself through college. If all goes well, I'll be able to take my fourth term at Bowdoin next fall. You are very kind to take me into your home. I promise to behave." Then he laughed, showing large white teeth.

The master took care to include me in his greeting. Grandpa and I stood at the head of the horse while Uncle and Mr. Lamb unloaded the carriage. They carried the melodeon into the parlor, toted a box of songbooks to the shed and left the master's Kennebecker on the stairs. I was invited to ride in the carriage when the men took the horse to the barn. The horse's name was Midnight and it was plain that her owner took great pride in her. He gave her a rubdown and curried her tail and mane before leading her to her stall beyond those of Brownie and Whitey. Brownie stretched out his head and nuzzled the black mare. Whitey also stretched out his head, but not to nuzzle. He gave the newcomer a sharp nip as though to say, "Who are you? We want no strangers here."

Otis gave Whitey a gentle slap and remarked, "Whitey is all nip and no bite and no kick. He really is as gentle as a kitten."

I felt that it was my turn to take part in the conversation and I chose to make a few remarks about Brownie: "Brownie is as gentle as a kitten, too. But you ought to see how quick he can kick a dashboard out of a buggy."

So while the master measured out oats for Midnight and gave her forkfuls of hay, Uncle Otis told the story of the bees at the Brown funeral.

After our supper of hasty pudding and milk, we sat in the parlor beside the Franklin stove, where a bright fire burned in honor of the master. Because it was Sunday the hands of my grandparents and uncle were idle. Grandma's held no needles; Uncle's and Grandpa's held neither paring nor carving knife. To begin our evening Grandmother asked our guest a question, "How does it happen that a young, good looking man like you is unmarried?"

His answer was, "I must finish my schooling before I think of getting married." Then he said, "Your question reminds me of a story."

We were to learn that questions were always reminding him of stories. Telling a story is a skill that is never learned. A man or woman is born with it and never loses it. As near as I can recall, this is how he told the story, the first of many that he told during his stay with us.

"About two years ago I went to York County to hold singing school in Newfield and Limerick. I had a good time and taught two real smart groups. Everywhere I went they told me about a music master from Durham, New Hampshire. The man was in the mid-thirties, had lost his wife, and was eager to remarry. So he advertised in a Portsmouth paper for a 'musical housekeeper.' Of course he had matrimony in mind but one cannot advertise for a wife in a respectable paper.

"There were several women who applied in person. One was too old, a second was too young, the third was so togged out with gewgaws that the master felt she would be an extravagant cook. He finally hired a woman from Vermont, sight unseen. He liked her hand writing, her age was right, she enclosed clippings from a Burlington paper that listed her as playing in the brass section of the Bennington band. In the summer the Durham master got together a band that played at various fairs and he decided that an extra cornet player was just what he needed.

"The musical housekeeper arrived in August. She came by train with her trunk, her cornet, and her French horn. The master and the housekeeper were so busy with their household plans that there was no time to discuss music. When the band met, however, the housekeeper blew mightily and tunefully on her cornet. Their first performance of September was at Parsonsfield Fair. The band went to the fair in long buckboards with their instruments under the buckboard seats. The leader gave to his housekeeper the sheets of music for the three members of the brass section.

"They were late in arriving at the fair grounds, and the crowd was waiting for the concert. Hurriedly the band members took their seats in the judges' stand; music was set on the racks. Because the crowd was so large the master told the brass section to play very loud. They did. The sound of the brass instruments brought the listeners to their feet, startled the race horses in their stalls, and set the cattle in the sheds to blatting. The musical housekeeper had given the trumpet music to the trombone player, the cornet music to the trumpet player and the trombone music to herself. She was playing by ear."

We all laughed at the master's story and Otis said, "I expect that the housekeeper was fired."

"No, indeed," replied Mr. Lamb, "Though she could not tell a sharp from a flat on paper, her ear was true. Though she could not read music, she could read a cookbook. The pies and the cakes and the turnovers that she baked were the talk of Durham. The fiasco at Parsonsfield Fair was forgiven and forgotten. The musical housekeeper was promoted to wife. But she never again played in the brass section."

After the story the master played the melodeon for us. Grandma was proud to tell him that Otis played the violin, the trumpet, and the drum. She took pains to add, "Our son reads music."

On weekdays Uncle Otis and the teacher gave us some gay tunes. Mother's oleander swayed in the musical breezes and Grandma moved her vases further back on the parlor shelf lest they be jarred to the floor.

Late Monday afternoon the master drove to the Head-of-the-Bay to organize his village class. He took with him his melodeon and the box of songbooks, bringing them back when he returned in the late evening. Things began well. Every morning at breakfast he told us how either Mr. Stevens or Mr. Holt looked in during the evening, how the enrollment increased each time, and that the Clough and Peters children had fine voices.

Things did not start as smoothly at McHeard's. On Thursday after an early supper, the master hitched Midnight to his loaded carriage and we left for the schoolhouse. I was proud to sit in the front seat with the master and the Closson girls. Joel and his brother Sam sat on the carriage floor in back of the seat and dangled their feet. The York and Means children joined us before we crossed the bridge over Uncle Joel's mill brook. When we reached the schoolhouse, we found some twenty children waiting for us. My playmates Sarah Miller and Cousin Clara were among them. The master shepherded us into the schoolroom, directed the big boys to bring in the books and the melodeon, and then proceded to sort us out.

He had already listened to the Clossons and me. He had kindly remarked on my voice; "Sweet, but weak." He had smiled and nodded when the Closson children sang. In the schoolhouse he stood in front of each child in turn and sang the scale:

Each sang back the notes to him. Soon the young ones were in such a giggle that he went outside and tested the children one by one.

At last we were divided into four groups, the treble, the alto, the tenor and the bass. Only Cousin George and the York boys sang bass; Joel and Sam were the best tenors. Clara, Sarah and I stood in the alto section. I shared a book with Clara. Our first song was "America." On the third verse Clara whispered to me, "Hannah, for Heaven's sake, make your voice go up or go down."

Clara did not like my singing. I did not like her talking when Mr. Lamb was attempting to teach us something. On the second night I shared my book with Sarah. She did not complain about my singing.

When we started our second song, we were startled by a shower of rocks hitting the front of the schoolhouse. The master and the big boys rushed out in time to see four or five young men running up the road toward Morgan's Bay. After they disappeared the master and pupils returned to the schoolroom and we started to sing the round "Scotland's Burning." Just as we were "pouring on water" there was an interruption. This time the rowdies were on the opposite corner singing ribald songs. For a second time they were driven toward home. The master had to dismiss the school early because of continued disturbances. We noticed that all the way home the master was very quiet.

On Friday morning we had early callers. Uncle Joel and Clara came before I had left for school, or the men for the fields. It was hard to tell which of our two callers was the more worked up. Uncle Joel was wringing his hands and Clara was almost crying. Both talked loudly and rapidly. Finally Grandmother got Clara to keep silent and her father to slow down. The gist of Uncle's grievance was that the reputation of McHeard's would be ruined if rowdies were allowed to break up the singing school. He proposed that he and Uncle Otis should go to Ellsworth to summon the sheriff to arrest the boys from Morgan's Bay.

Mr. Lamb listened quietly, gave his thanks, but refused Uncle's suggestion. He said, "This is my problem. I have had similar ones before. I believe that I can work it out. Otis tells me that the boys from Morgan's Bay have had few advantages. Likely they feel left out. We shall see."

On Friday evening when we drove to McHeard's, a second carriage followed the master's. The carriage was drawn by Brownie and in it were Uncle Otis, Mr. Closson, and Mr. Grindle. Both horses were unhitched, unharnessed and led into the long barn. The three men went into Aunt Abigail's kitchen. The master and we children went to the schoolhouse.

Friday night's disturbance was a repetition of Thursday's but with a different ending. This time, when the boys ran toward home they were surprised and seized by Uncle Joel and the three men from the Corner who had been watching for them from the kitchen. The boys were some shocked and not a little frightened. Uncle Joel started to threaten them but the master would have none of that. "Boys," he said, "I am going to make you a proposition. Last night I heard you sing. I did not like your songs. I did like your voices. I invite you to be in the singing school and join the bass section. We have only three in it. We need you."

Released by their captors and taken by surprise at the invitation, the Morgan's Bay boys did not know what to say. The two younger ones wheeled about and leg-bailed it toward home. The leader smoothed his hair, put his shirt tail in his pantaloons, spit out his cud of tobacco and said, "Well, I don't care if we do."

That was the end of the trouble. The spokesman and his two friends joined the bass section; the next night the two younger boys came back to the school and were placed with the tenors. The singing school ended with an outdoor concert that featured a song by the five basses, "Safely Through Another Week." Uncle Otis's comment was, "Ought to be, 'safely through another school.'"

The singing master taught evenings; he prepared for his teaching afternoons; he helped with the farm work mornings. He insisted on cleaning out the three horse stalls. Whatever Grandfather and Uncle did, he did. One week they were planting grain—rye and buckwheat in the middle field, corn and wheat in the upper field. On the first morning Mr. Lamb said to Uncle, "I believe that grain can best be planted to music. Let me think of some appropriate songs."

Grandfather recalled how the two young men sowed seed to the rhythm of song. Most often they sang the hymn,

> All that spring with beauteous hand,
> Scatters o'er the smiling land,

All that plenteous Summer pours,
Autumn's rich o'er flowing stores,
Lord, for these our souls shall raise
Grateful vows and solemn praise.

The second week, the men dropped potatoes in the lower field. Potatoes should be planted to the tune of Irish songs, the master decided. We children hurried home from school every afternoon to help out with the planting and to join in the singing. One afternoon the workers took time off to play with the children and the master taught us to do Irish jigs. Friday evening, Uncle Zenas called at the house and said to Grandfather, "Well, Mr. Friend, I notice your potatoes are all sung-in. I wish that your crew would come over tomorrow to my shore meadow and help me jig-in my turnips." That was exactly what we did.

All the Friend family liked John Lamb. Otis enjoyed his music most, but my grandparents and I especially liked his stories. Some of the master's yarns were amusing. He told of boarding at one place where the cat slept in the flour barrel on cold nights. He liked to tell about the exacting grandfather who was always picking up after his son and daughter-in-law. One afternoon the son left a bag of dynamite caps on the kitchen table. The grandpa thought that the bag was empty and he threw it in the kitchen stove. He had been deaf for a decade. That afternoon he heard, and he felt a glancing blow from a stove lid as it flew by him.

One of his stories was sad. He told it one noontime when Grandma remarked that her white geranium would likely be in bloom for Decoration Day. He was reminded of the spring that he spent with a prosperous couple in mid-Maine. The children were grown; only one, the youngest, remained at home with the old folks. There had been eight children, four sons and four daughters. The children had been prone to typhoid fever. Two of the daughters, both teachers, had died of the fever in nearby towns and been buried in the neighborhood burying ground. Two of the sons had died far from home, one in Michigan and one in Massachusetts. Their bodies were not brought home for burial and so their parents did not have the comfort of visiting their graves.

When the sons had been boys, they had amused themselves by chipping their names on rock. Walter had cut his name on the corner foundation stone of his father's shop. Clifford had carved his on a moss-covered stone at the head of the field. On Decoration Day the parents took flowers to the family lot in the cemetery and then they visited the stones of Walter and Clifford where they left bouquets. The master recalled that he went with them. "I knelt to place the flowers on the daughters' graves and again to place bouquets by the rocks that the sons had cut. At Clifford's rock I sang a hymn. The three of us faced west. There were a good many Maine boys who went west in the 1830s and 1840s who never came home."

One of the teacher's stories was really gruesome. One August he had boarded in a home of a village where he was teaching a singing school. After the evening session was over, he liked to stop at the store where there was always a group of loafers. The storekeeper was an old man who had once gone to sea. He took great pride in his produce brought in from the Islands and in his sign, which read, W.I. GOODS (West Indies goods). In the summer he had fruit brought in by steamboat from Boston. This evening the master lingered to listen to the stories. When he left the Captain gave him a basket of grapes, and said, "There are only two baskets left. You take this one with you. I'm going to take the other one home to my wife."

The master gave his thanks, left the store and crossed the plank bridge over the mill brook to his boarding place. At midnight he was wakened by his host, "Get up, get up, Master. The storekeeper is missing. He never showed up at home. Come join the searchers."

The storekeeper's body was found in the mill brook. He had been stabbed and his money had been taken. Evidently there had been a struggle on the bridge; the basket of grapes had been upset and the grapes trampled by the "Captain" and his murderer. There was the purple of grapes and the red of blood on the wooden planking of the bridge. The murderer was identified by the stains on his shoes.

This story made a great impression on me. Several years later when Clara and I were at Sarah's house, we tired of our dolls. I suggested that we enact the murder of the storekeeper. The plank bridge over Uncle Joel's mill brook was a perfect stage. We took care with our preparations. We picked string cherries and pressed them for "blood." We picked blueberries to substitute for the purple grapes. We gathered flat rocks for the Captain's money. We found a salt bag to serve as a money bag. After all the preparations, the play nearly fell through because there was no part that Clara wanted to play. She could not bring herself to be the killer; she certainly did not wish to be killed; she never would have dared to search for the corpse. Finally we assured her that the murder would be swift and painless and she consented to be the victim.

The murder was painless but not stainless, and Clara's pink apron was covered with "grape stains" and "blood." Clara was a highly satisfactory victim. Her screams rent the air. Fortunately the sound of the mill deadened her cries so that neither her father nor mother heard her. The three of us were so pleased with our production that we repeated it for the benefit of Clara's brothers.

Our playacting had an aftermath. Clara had nightmares and for the duration of the summer would not cross the bridge alone after dark. Uncle Joel blamed me and was all for having me punished. But Aunt Abigail took my part, "Hannah has a high imagination. There is no harm in acting. Clara should have more imagination."

I can't say that I learned much about music from Mr. Lamb. But of course there is no music in me. But he did teach me much about storytelling. He used to say, "A storyteller has the license to alter and embroider. For the sake of telling a good story he may stretch the truth a leetle."

The Stover Sisters

When I was eleven years old I made new friends—the Stover Sisters, Emma and Joanne, who had been brought up on Calf Island off Sorrento. Emma, the older, came to the Corner to look after Mrs. Closson, who was poorly. Mrs. Closson needed nursing; Uncle Zenas and the boys needed someone to mend and cook for them; the two little girls, Kate and Hattie, needed someone to mother them. Emma was beautiful: tall, slender, and blond. She was modest and she seldom spoke. She comforted Mrs. Closson; she reassured Uncle Zenas, and she mothered the children. She brought Joanne with her.

Joanne was twelve years old. She had brown hair and eyes, and was short and stalwart. She was not modest and she spoke often. Joanne was always telling me, "You know that I am the youngest of six sisters and by far the smartest." She was a great one to quote her mother and often remarked, "My mother says that I am the smartest of her six daughters."

Certainly Joanne had grounds for her pride. She could knit and crochet and tat. She could hook rugs and quilt bed coverings. She could preserve and cook and make soap. She could drive a horse and milk a cow. She could fish and hunt and row a boat.

Indeed, Joanne was an artist with oars. Her stroke was strong and even; she could even row cross-handed. She could move the boat above a bar or inches from a shore boulder and not scrape the paint.

One day Joanne took the Baptist minister and his wife and me out fishing. Parson Briggs and his wife came often to the Friend farmhouse. Grandma and Grandpa were delighted when they came but Uncle Otis was not as cordial. He used to say, "I notice that they always show up just at dinner time."

On the incoming tide Joanne rowed us away from the home shore around Porgy Point to Closson's Point, where Uncle Zenas and his boys were planting turnips in the garden. Beyond Closson's Point we stopped at the Grindle wharf to watch Mr. Saunders and Mr. Grindle unload paving from a jigger.

I liked to brag about Mr. Grindle and so I said, "Our neighbor, Mr. Grindle, is very smart. Grandpa says that he has a lot of money in the bank. He gave Elva and Emma each a gold piece when they were born."

Parson Briggs made a crisp comment, "He ought to come to church more often."

When I repeated the conversation to Uncle Otis, he said, "The parson was thinking of a gold piece in the collection bag."

Off Sculpin Point we caught flounders. When Joanne turned the boat for the row home, she found that the tide was still running in and that the wind was against us. The rowing was hard. I offered to help Joanne but the parson didn't. Uncle Otis had been mending porgy nets in the boat house. When he saw what hard work Joanne was having he rowed out in the peapod, fastened the peapod to the row boat, clambered aboard the boat and rowed us to shore. When we neared the beach, Uncle jumped out, pulled up the boat, and carefully helped Mrs. Briggs and Joanne and me ashore. The parson was the last. As he jumped, a wave hit the boat; he lost his footing and landed in the water. Mrs. Briggs lamented; Joanne and I giggled; Uncle apologized. Parson Briggs said nothing and looked very sober as he squeezed water from his pants legs. It was several weeks before he and his wife came again to visit at the Corner.

Uncle Otis liked to tell the story of the parson's wetting. He always ended his account with a little ditty:

> The parson came
> To catch a flounder.
> It was a shame
> He had to founder.

Grandmother always gently reproved him, "Now, Son, it is not becoming to poke fun at a parson." But I noticed that the corners of her mouth twitched.

One day Uncle Zenas and Emma went to the Head-of-the-Bay to buy calico and medicines for Mrs. Closson. They bought gifts for all the children: Gibralters for Joel and Sam; lozenges for Will and the little girls; cross-stitch paper and colored thread for Joanne and me.

Emma promised to teach Joanne and me how to cross-stitch. Joanne conceded, "That's one thing that I do not know how to do. But I'll learn fast enough. In no time I'll be cross-stitching better than Emma."

Once Joanne and I learned the stitch we had to decide upon a design. I settled for a beflowered harp with the word "music" above it. Joanne was more ambitious. She chose a design of purple lilacs and consulted her friends about a proper motto. Grandma suggested "Love Truth." Mrs. Closson favored "God is Love." The boys were all for a patriotic motto such as "Liberty and Union" or "United We Stand."

But Joanne embroidered the motto that Uncle Zenas suggested. When the lilacs were done and the motto in place, every stitch even and identical, Uncle Zenas framed the piece for her and Joel hung it above her bed. The motto was, "Let another man praise thee." When Joanne told Grandmother about the motto, Grandma said, "Yes, that comes from Proverbs."

"Yes," agreed Joanne, "It comes from the second verse of the twenty-seventh chapter. Uncle Zenas asked me to memorize the entire verse and I have."

"Then let's say it together," said Grandmother. "Let another man praise thee, and not thine own mouth; a stranger and not thine own lips."

After that, when Grandfather or David criticized Joanne, Grandmother always defended her. "Of course Joanne is prideful because she is so smart. She will grow up to be as modest as Emma and likely as beautiful. Children ain't all alike. A hen and a bumble bee can't be fetched up alike."

One afternoon Aunt Abigail Long and Mrs. Miller came to call on Grandmother. When they had not gone home by four o'clock, it was evident they planned to stay to supper. I knew that there were only fish hash and gingerbread for supper. When I confided to Joanne the state of the larder, she said, "Go whisper to your grandmother not to worry; that you and I are going to get supper."

While Joanne made biscuits I stirred up a two-egg cake. While Joanne watched the baking of the biscuits and the cake and browned the hash on the top of the stove, I went to the bushes above the sheep pen for raspberries.

At my suggestion we set the table for the ladies in the bedroom. We spread a linen cloth on a tea table and set the table with the gold-banded dishes. Then we set the table in the kitchen for Grandfather, Uncle and the boys. When David came into the kitchen, he exclaimed, "I vum! Something smells mighty good."

When supper was all ready, Joanne said, "I'll have to fly or Emma will start to worry. You need not let the McHeard ladies know that I helped you."

When supper was over I heard one of Grandmother's guests say, "I had no idea that Hannah was so capable."

I hurried right in to remark, "But Joanne Stover helped me."

And that led to the question "Who is Joanne Stover?"

Grandma said, "A capable girl just like my Hannah."

There were other comments in the kitchen. David said, "Joanne is the most talkative girl in town." Grandpa said, "A girl who is improving every day." Otis said, "That is right, Father. Some day she may be as nice as her sister Emma."

One afternoon Joanne and I walked toward McHeard's to gather roadside herbs that Grandmother used in her medicines. Painter went with us. We picked the fernlike leaves of yarrow which grandmother boiled with molasses to make cough syrup. We gathered boneset, with its white flowers and jointed stalks. Mixed with camphorated oil, the leaves make a lotion that helps lameness. We dug up the roots of mullein. These were used to make a medicine against chills. We went into a woodside grove to pull up the roots of bloodroot that Grandma brewed to make a tonic.

On our way coming home we met Cousin George Long returning from an errand at the Head-of-the-Bay. He pulled up the horse and asked us to ride a piece with him. Quick as a wink, Joanne hopped over the wheel and sat beside him. I doubted that Grandma would wish me to leave the neighborhood so late in the afternoon but I decided to follow Joanne's example. Painter had other ideas: when I attempted to get in the carriage, he barked and nudged me away from the vehicle. Joanne and George shouted at him, "Painter, go home," but he growled at them. The horse became excited and pulled on the reins. George shouted, "Whoa, whoa there!" Painter growled and barked all the more.

Uncle Otis, who was coming home from work in the back field, heard all the noise and came running. Painter and I were glad to see him, but not George and Joanne. Uncle listened to George's explanation and then he said to Joanne, "You had better jump out and get home. Emma will be needing you."

Joanne was quick to obey. As she started to jump from the carriage, the horse moved ahead and she caught her foot in the wheel. She fell in the road, her hands became bloody and begrimed. Uncle and George knelt to examine her ankle. Unwatched, the horse started for home and had to be chased and brought back. Joanne winked back the tears and exclaimed, "Oh dear! there is a rip in my skirt."

"But plainly your ankle is not broken," said Uncle Otis. He lifted Joanne into the carriage and sat beside her while George backed the horse and carriage and started to drive to Closson's. Painter and I trudged behind in the cloud of dust made by the carriage. The basket of herbs was left forgotten by the roadside until supper when David went for it.

When we got to our house, Uncle sent me in to tell the folks about the accident. Grandfather was cross and said, "George had no business to ask the girls to ride, and Joanne should have known better than to get into the carriage. Painter knew more than she did."

Grandmother was more charitable, "Now, John," she said, "Joanne is only a child. Neither she nor George meant any harm."

After Grandpa went to the barn I heard Grandma say to David, "It was Otis who was at fault. It would have done no harm if Joanne had gone to ride with George. Hannah and Painter could have come home without her."

When Joanne recovered from her accident she was quieter. She seldom quoted her mother and never referred to her own skills. Grandfather paid her the high compliment of saying, "She now begins to be a little like Emma."

Uncle Otis said nothing, but he smiled at Grandfather's comment. He was always pleased when anyone praised Emma.

By September, Mrs. Closson was well, and the Stovers sent word for their daughters to come home. Everyone at the Corner hated to see the Stover sisters leave. Mrs. Closson and her little girls wept. Grandmother and Mrs. Grindle gave each of the sisters a gift. Grandfather suggested that Otis take the girls home in his sail boat, and Otis consented. Both Joel and Sam wanted to go along for the trip to Calf Island, but my grandfather with unusual curtness said, "No, boys. Not this time."

That evening, while I was reading in the parlor I heard a conversation between my grandparents.

Grandparents asked, "Why did you discourage the boys from going with Otis?"

Replied my grandfather, "I wanted to make sure that Otis would have a chance to ask Emma."

It was a conversation that I did not understand. I wanted to rush to the kitchen and inquire, "Ask Emma what?" But something kept me from going.

The next day the sun shone; the wind blew lightly from the west. It was just the day for a sail to Calf Island. Otis and the sisters left at seven o'clock. Uncle's last words were reassuring: "I'll be home by early evening. I expect a shift of wind in the afternoon."

Before seven o'clock Grandma and I saw Uncle walking up the field from the shore and we heard his whistle. Said Grandmother, "Let's go to meet him, Hannah. Perhaps he has good news for us."

Accompanied by Painter, we crossed the road and went across the field to meet Uncle. Uncle shouted at the dog and called to us, "What's for supper? I'm starved." He quickened his step and was soon beside us.

When Grandma took her stepson's arm she said, "Do you have good news for us about yourself and Emma?"

"Yes indeed," said Uncle, "I have good news about myself and Emma and Joanne. We got to the island safely and both girls were mighty glad to be home."

It was evident that Otis himself was glad to be at home. All during supper he laughed more than usual. In the evening he got out his trumpet and played lively marches. But my grandfather and grandmother said very little. In fact, they seemed to be disappointed over something.

After I had undressed, said my prayers and gone to bed I thought about Emma and Joanne. I said to myself, "I shall never see them again." A few tears flowed down my cheeks and wet the pillow.

Afterword

Readers may wish to know what happened to Hannah, her family and friends after 1855.

In 1860 a son was born to Giles and Eliza Wood. He was named Arthur Brooks for a first mate who was drowned when the schooner capsized. The Captain and his wife built a home on the land that they purchased from John Friend. A second son was born in 1866 and he was named for Eliza's father. Arthur had three children who survived him. He has many descendants. I am the child of John Friend Wood and his only descendant.

When Hannah was sixteen years old, she went to Dover, New Hampshire where she worked in a coat shop. When she came home for a visit she met Octave Paradise, a French-Canadian who had come to Blue Hill to work in the granite yards. She married him in 1862 and to please her he changed his name to Howard. Hannah and Octave first lived in Bucksport, then at Friend's Corner, in Burlington, Vermont and finally in Rockland. They had four sons, all of whom have descendants.

Otis Friend did marry. I hope that readers will be surprised to learn that he married Joanne and not the beautiful Emma so admired by his father and step-mother. Otis built a home for himself and his bride on land given him by his father. Otis and Joanne had two daughters. Both married and had children. Otis enlisted to fight in the Civil War and died in a hospital in Virginia.

It is with hesitation that I write about John Stillman Friend. Aunt Hannah and her brothers seldom mentioned him. One year when his ship, a Portsmouth, New Hampshire craft, returned from China with a load of tea and calicoes for the port of Salem, Mate John Friend was not aboard. The captain wrote Rebecca that her husband was left behind in China because he was dying from cholera. The Friends and Rebecca mourned and Rebecca wore black. Several years later a man from Sedgwick returned from California and reported that he had met John Friend on a street in San Francisco. He said of the man, "He denied that he was John Friend of Blue Hill. But he looked like him and his voice was like his." Aunt Hannah always asserted, "Of course the man from Sedgwick was wrong. Certainly Uncle John died in China." Uncle Arthur's assertion was very different, "It may well have been that John Stillman decided to shift from forecastle to mine shaft."

Flavilla married Emery Herrick of Brooksville. She and her husband changed the family home into a boarding house and took summer boarders. Some of her descendants still run the hotel that Flavilla named the Oakland House.

Both Joel Closson and Moses Long lost their lives in the Civil War. Zenas Closson refused to take the government pension that was his due from Joel's death. Will Closson, an adopted son, was the comfort of Uncle Zenas's old age.

Milford Grindle's last years were sad. His wife died when her fifth child was born. He was prosperous but he was always concerned about the problems of his children.

The John Friend house, greatly changed, still stands as does the home of Otis Friend. The long, rambling house built by Captain Giles Wood burned in the 1920's. The homes of Zenas Closson and Milford Grindle still stand as does the barn in which once lived Old Gyp and the quarry oxen. The doorstep of the old schoolhouse is still in place. Walls built by Friend's Corner farmers remain; wood roads cut by them are still in use.

Local geography keeps alive the names of Hannah's family and neighbors. We have Friend's Corner and Darling Island and Wood Point and Closson Point.

Acknowledgements

I appreciate the help that I have received with Hannah's stories. Lawrence Dodge helped me with the barn raising; Murray Tapley, with details of country living; William Hinckley, with the preparation of the map; Captain Robert Slaven, with the building of the *Meridian*. Virginia Perkins gave me good advice. Nina Bailey of Gorham provided the music for Otis's songs. Karen Womer of West Rockport edited the stories.

Nathalie Edwards, one of Hannah's great-granddaughters, provided the picture of Hannah.

Emily Bartlett, one of Hannah's great-great-nieces, drew the design used at the end of the last chapter.

About the Author

Esther E. Wood was a descendant of pre-1790 settlers who came to Ellsworth, Orland, Penobscot, Deer Isle, Sedgwick, Brooksville, and Blue Hill, Maine. A graduate of Stevens Academy in 1922 and Colby College in 1926, she received a master's degree from Radcliffe in 1929 and an honorary degree from Colby College in 1972. She taught history on the same hillside campus in Gorham, Maine, for forty-two years.

She wrote about her childhood at Friend's Corner for *The Christian Science Monitor's* "Home Forum Page" and also wrote monthly pieces for *New England Homestead, Down East, Maine Life, Woman's Day* and the Maine Sunday papers. Her column for the *Ellsworth American,* "The Native," ran for over twenty years.

Her other published books are *Country Fare: Reminiscences and Recipes From a Maine Childhood* (New Hampshire Publishing, 1976), *Saltwater Seasons: Recollections of a Country Woman* (Down East Books, 1980), and *Deep Roots: A Maine Legacy* (Yankee Books, 1990).

Esther Wood died at her home at Friend's Corner, East Blue Hill, in 2002 at the age of 97.

Genealogy House

Publishers of Family History and Genealogy

Genealogy House publishes narrative family histories and genealogies that combine good writing and editing with genealogical research.

By incorporating high editorial and production standards, we maintain the best of traditional publishing and combine it with today's advantages of digital printing and distribution technologies. The result is a process that is professional, efficient, cost effective, flexible, and responsible.

Our goal is to capture the spirit of the people of the past to share with generations to come.

A division of White River Press
Amherst, Massachusetts

genealogyhouse.net

CPSIA information can be obtained at www.ICGtesting.com
Printed in the USA
BVOW03s1553050614

355342BV00001B/2/P